"Geoffrey James, the best writer in the B2B sales business, has gathered compelling, relevant, and thoroughly field-tested content from the experts in fifteen critical B2B selling areas and served them up for you in a powerful, organized, and deliciously consumable way. If you're in sales or sales management, you're going to *love* this book."   **—Dave Stein, CEO and founder of ES Research Group**

"This amazing book offers great sales nuggets that can help B2B salespeople improve their skills, expand their confidence, increase their income, and drive up customer loyalty. A must-read for newly hired salespeople and a great refresher for the seasoned pro."   **—Gerhard Gschwandtner, publisher of *Selling Power* magazine**

"Geoffrey James has an unusual and distinct advantage as an author: (1) He's been a reporter, with deep access into his beat, and the wisdom to use this resource to select the best from each. (2) He's a versatile and well-rounded business observer with active involvement in information technology, marketing, sales and the broader art of networking, and, of course, publishing. (3) He's been a writer with a following of a half million readers a month who are more than willing to 'correct' his observations of the sales world. And finally, (4) he knows how to write . . . simply and directly!"

—Howard Stevens, CEO of HR Chally

"Geoffrey James knows salespeople. He's written a short, pithy book with real-time examples that resonate—no matter what we sell. Read this book and you not only will sell smarter, but you will increase your success rate ten-fold. Geoffrey removes sales fears and puts the fun back in sales."   **—Joanne Black, founder of No More Cold Calling**

"In a world where bookshelves are packed with intricate advice and complex selling models, Geoffrey's book delivers a fresh perspective around the natural yet powerful simplicity of the selling process—from crafting a winning sales strategy to developing the skill set of a top producer. Rather than overcomplicate and overanalyze, *How to Say It: Business to Business Selling* provides practical solutions that any salesperson can quickly digest and leverage today."

—Keith Rosen, author of *Coaching Salespeople into Sales Champions*

continued . . .

"Followers of Geoffrey's blog, *Sales Machine*, know salespeople are made and not born. If you want to take apart a sales machine and see what makes it tick, this book is for you. You'll be up and running and on the fast track in no time."

—Linda Richardson, founder and executive chairwoman of Richardson

"I like this book. The world needs a basic manual for B2B selling."

—Mike Bosworth, author of *Solution Selling*

"To build a portfolio of B2B accounts requires in-depth knowledge that can be worth the effort and time to acquire. Geoffrey's work is a valuable addition to the tools that are available to the budding B2B expert."

—Robert Carr, CEO of Heartland Payment Systems

"Geoff has taken the mystery out of business to business selling by providing pragmatic advice and insights. People brand-new to selling as well as seasoned veterans will learn how to be more effective salespeople and improve their ability to build long-term customer relationships." **—Sam Reese, CEO of Miller Heiman**

"Geoffrey James does a superb job of bringing to life the keys to successful selling for those who are new to the profession of selling as well as those who have been selling for decades. If you are a sales coach, sales leader, or salesperson, this book is a must-read." **—Sharon M. Daniels, CEO of AchieveGlobal**

HOW TO SAY IT
Business to Business Selling

Power Words and Strategies
from the World's Top Sales Experts

GEOFFREY JAMES

Prentice Hall Press

PRENTICE HALL PRESS
Published by the Penguin Group
Penguin Group (USA) Inc.
375 Hudson Street, New York, New York 10014, USA
Penguin Group (Canada), 90 Eglinton Avenue East, Suite 700, Toronto, Ontario M4P 2Y3, Canada
(a division of Pearson Penguin Canada Inc.)
Penguin Books Ltd., 80 Strand, London WC2R 0RL, England
Penguin Group Ireland, 25 St. Stephen's Green, Dublin 2, Ireland (a division of Penguin Books Ltd.)
Penguin Group (Australia), 250 Camberwell Road, Camberwell, Victoria 3124, Australia
(a division of Pearson Australia Group Pty. Ltd.)
Penguin Books India Pvt. Ltd., 11 Community Centre, Panchsheel Park, New Delhi—110 017, India
Penguin Group (NZ), 67 Apollo Drive, Rosedale, Auckland 0632, New Zealand
(a division of Pearson New Zealand Ltd.)
Penguin Books (South Africa) (Pty.) Ltd., 24 Sturdee Avenue, Rosebank, Johannesburg 2196,
South Africa

Penguin Books Ltd., Registered Offices: 80 Strand, London WC2R 0RL, England

While the author has made every effort to provide accurate telephone numbers and Internet addresses at the time of publication, neither the publisher nor the author assumes any responsibility for errors or for changes that occur after publication. Further, the publisher does not have any control over and does not assume any responsibility for author or third-party websites or their content.

First edition: December 2011

Library of Congress Cataloging-in-Publication Data

James, Geoffrey, 1953–
   How to say it : business to business selling : power words and strategies from the world's top sales experts / Geoffrey James.— 1st ed.
      p.   cm.
   ISBN 978-0-7352-0458-4
   1. Industrial marketing.   2. Business communication.   3. Selling.   I. Title.
   HF5415.1263.J36   2011
   658.8'04—dc22   2011030654

PRINTED IN THE UNITED STATES OF AMERICA

10 9 8 7 6 5 4 3 2 1

Most Prentice Hall Press books are available at special quantity discounts for bulk purchases for sales promotions, premiums, fund-raising, or educational use. Special books, or book excerpts, can also be created to fit specific needs. For details, write: Special Markets, Penguin Group (USA) Inc., 375 Hudson Street, New York, New York 10014.

This book is dedicated to my friend and mentor
Gerhard Gschwandtner, publisher of Selling Power *magazine.*

ACKNOWLEDGMENTS

I'd like to thank my editor at Prentice Hall Press, Maria Gagliano. I originally handed her a manuscript that was little more than a collection of blog posts. She saw there was much more that I could do with the material and insisted that I make it more useful, with more examples and a more logical structure. I will be forever grateful that she was patient enough to make this book the best I could possibly make it. I also want to thank my agent, Lorin Rees, for helping me prepare the book proposal and for making sure that it got Maria's attention.

Over the years, I've interviewed dozens of sales gurus, and their thoughts are naturally reflected in this book. Some of them were so influential that I've identified them in the text. However, for the sake of completeness, here are my heroes, the sales trainers and thinkers of the world: Tom Hopkins (handling objections), Brian Tracy (effective presentations), Linda Richardson (closing sales, management coaching, and competitive selling), Ron Willingham (psychology of sales), Mike Bosworth (solution selling), Randall Murphy (sales negotiations and consultative selling), Sam Reese (strategic accounts), Tom Sant (effective proposals), Jeff Gitomer (customer referrals), Jeff Seeley (sales process), Neil Rackham (access to decision makers), Earl Taylor (building rapport), Rob Scher (emotional intelligence), Tom Roth (pinpointing good prospects), Robert Cialdini (influencing customers), Art Mortell (handling rejection), Jeff Keller (positive attitude), Omar Periu (getting motivated), Wayne Turmel (effective questioning), Joanne Black (referral selling), Jerry Acuff (building customer relationships), Mark Shonka and Dan Kosch (selling at the C-level), Sharon Daniels (setting sales priorities), Wendy Weiss (cold calling), Jim Holden (international sales), Waldo "Wingman" (sales missions), Michael St. Lawrence (seeing for results), Bill Stinnett (customer results), Andrea Sittig-Rolf (cold calling), Jeff Thull (high-stakes selling), Howard Stevens (world-class selling), Steve Martin (heavy-hitter selling), Phil Geldart (building teamwork), Greg Winograd (following through), Terri Sjodin (persuasive presentations), Julie Thomas (adapting to customers), John Asher (correcting sales mistakes), Duane Sparks (breaking sales records), Donal Daly (reducing sales costs), Tom Black (simplifying sales processes), Thomas Ray Crowel (power prospecting), Barry Rhein (elevator pitches), Ed Rigsbee (sales partnering), Dean Schantz (power of story), Dean Brenner (effective communications), Mark Sellers (sales funnel), Robert Nadeau (defending prices), Keith Rosen (qualifying prospects), Ryan Kubacki (selling intuitively), Sharon Daniels (complex sales), and Nancy Martini (customer-centric selling).

I'd like to give special thanks to Gerhard Gschwandtner, the publisher of *Selling Power* magazine and his wife, Laura, the editor. They got me started writing about selling and have provided an incredible amount of advice and guidance.

Finally, there are the folk at BNET who have been so patient with me when the blog first started and who have helped me make it so successful over the years. BNET is a huge undertaking, so it would be impossible to thank everyone personally, but specifically I'd like to thank Christine Lee, Eric Schurenberg, Paul Sloan, Karen Steen, and Stephen Howard-Sarin.

CONTENTS

Introduction.. xiii

Part One: How to Generate B2B Sales Leads

1. How to Write an Effective Sales Message 3
2. How to Get Sales Leads Through Referrals................................19
3. How to Get Sales Leads Through Networking 27
4. How to Get Sales Leads Through Partnerships 43
5. How to Get Sales Leads from the Internet 51

Part Two: How to Fill Your B2B Sales Pipeline

6. How to Motivate Yourself to Sell...65
7. How to Have Initial Conversations...75
8. How to Prospect Using Voicemail..89
9. How to Cope with Rejection While Prospecting.....................95
10. How to Convert a Lead into a Prospect...............................103

Part Three: How to Develop a B2B Opportunity

11. How to Define Your B2B Sales Campaign...111

12. How to Build Consensus to Buy..119

13. How to Give a B2B Sales Presentation..131

14. How to Give a B2B Product Demonstration...141

15. How to Write a Sales Proposal 149

Part Four: How to Close a B2B Deal

16. How to Close a B2B Sale...163

17. How to Negotiate Final Terms..171

18. How to Measure, Monitor, and Improve..179

HOW TO SAY IT
Business to Business Selling

INTRODUCTION

I'm not a sales guru and I don't do sales training. Since most how-to sales books are written by sales gurus and sales trainers, you might be wondering why I have written one.

Think of me as the world's first and only "sales fanboy." For reasons I don't quite understand, I find the behaviors and concepts involved in selling to be endlessly fascinating. I'm especially intrigued by B2B selling, which I consider the heart and soul of the business world.

As a result of my obsession, I've interviewed dozens of sales experts and trainers, discussed sales technique and sales management with hundreds of sales managers, and traded ideas about B2B selling with thousands of sales professionals.

Some of this activity has taken place through my relationship with *Selling Power* magazine, where I've been writing about sales technology and sales training for almost a decade. However, the place where I end up hashing out these things the most is my *Sales Machine* blog. As of this writing, *Sales Machine* is arguably the world's most popular sales-oriented blog, generating well in excess of a million page views a month. It's also won a couple of prestigious awards: a "Best in Business" from the Society of American Business Editors and Writers and an "Azbee" from the American Society of Business Publication Editors.

In the *Sales Machine* blog, I share what I learn about B2B selling with tens of thousands of B2B sales professionals, many of whom contribute their own content and ideas, in the form of comments and guest posts.

Over the years, I've written a number of blog posts that sales professionals in B2B firms have really found useful, based on the number of pageviews, comments, and email. For the past two years, *Sales Machine* readers have been pestering me to gather the best techniques into a single place, where they can be used for reference and as sales training tools.

This book, however, is more than just a collection of blog posts. I've expanded every technique and concept that was discussed in the blog, adding more examples, especially those from real-life situations, sent to me by real-life B2B sales pros.

The result is a document that is unique in the world of business books. Most books about selling treat selling to companies as if it were fundamentally the same as selling to consumers. But that's not true. B2B selling is vastly different, because:

- **Reason 1: The B2B buyer is vastly more sophisticated.** Because the Internet makes comparative pricing information publicly available, it is not at all unusual for a buyer in a B2B transaction to know more about the product category and the competition than the sales professionals who are trying to sell that type of product.

- **Reason 2: The stakes are much higher.** B2B buyers and decision makers are being paid high salaries to understand what they're buying and how it will be used. They can lose career points and get fired if they make a wrong decision, something that never happens when a consumer purchases a lousy consumer product.

- **Reason 3: B2B selling requires more knowledge.** When you're selling to businesses, it's not enough to understand a product and be able to present it coherently. B2B selling generally involves diagnosing a customer's challenges and then coming up with a customized solution that may very well involve a long-term business partnership.

- **Reason 4: B2B selling demands better people skills.** When consumers buy a product, typically there are only one or two decision makers involved (like a husband and wife). Corporate buying decisions can involve dozens of decision makers, influences, stakeholders, and naysayers. It takes extraordinary abilities to work with many different types of people, all of whom have different agendas.

- **Reason 5: B2B selling involves more patience.** Even big-ticket consumer sales (like homes and cars) can be completed in a day or a week (at most). By contrast, B2B deals can involve weeks and months of intermittent activity, meetings, phone calls, back-and-forth documents, as the deal moves through the customer bureaucracy.

- **Reason 6: B2B selling is more sensitive to economic disruption.** One of the first things that take place in an economic crisis is that firms lock down purchasing, add more layers of decision making, and demand concessions from their vendors. This takes place even for deals that have already been signed, and such tactics derail even the best-designed sales campaign.

- **Reason 7: B2B selling involves large sums of money.** In consumer sales, million-dollar deals are unusual and limited primarily to luxury homes. In B2B selling, by contrast, deals that involve millions of dollars are so commonplace as to be unremarkable. Even billion-dollar deals are struck from time to time. The stakes are high.

Even so, B2B selling is not complicated, if you know how the process works. That's what this book explains. It contains everything that you need to know to build and hone your B2B selling skills. I'm hoping it will be part of the library of every B2B salesperson—not just because I wrote it, but because I truly believe it provides the groundwork for a successful career in B2B sales.

Each of the book's four parts corresponds to a different stage of the selling process:

Part One explains how to generate great sales leads. It will help you identify lists of executives and managers who have the potential to become your prospects and (hopefully) your customers.

Part Two explains how to contact those sales leads and how to turn them into prospects that are in your sales pipeline.

Part Three explains how to develop an account once you've gotten your proverbial "foot in the door" by building consensus among groups of decision makers.

Part Four explains how to close the deal, negotiate the best terms, deal with the inevitable setbacks, and hone your overall approach.

Within each part are several chapters that provide the basic skills, in the order in which you should learn them. Each chapter also identifies additional resources and individuals who can help you perfect that skill.

I may not be a sales guru, but I know plenty of sales gurus, and I'm more than happy to send you to them, once you've mastered the basic techniques in this book.

Tell them I sent you, okay?

PART ONE

How to Generate B2B Sales Leads

The foundation of any B2B selling effort is sales leads, the raw material from which you make prospects (potential customers).

The key to finding sales leads is knowing exactly what you're selling, and how that appeals to your potential customers. That's why Chapter 1 teaches you an absolutely essential skill: how to write your sales message.

That sales message allows you to differentiate between good and bad leads. It also forms the core of your elevator pitch, your cold calling script, your voicemails, and even your major sales presentation. So pay close attention to Chapter 1. It's the foundation of your B2B sales career.

Once you're happy with your sales message, you'll learn how to get good sales leads in four different ways:

- **Referrals:** Getting your friends, colleagues, existing customers, and business contacts to refer their peers to you. You'll learn how to do this in Chapter 2.

- **Networking:** Meeting people who might be potential customers at industry events (and other occasions). You'll learn how to do this in Chapter 3.

- **Sales partnerships:** Working with other sales professionals in other companies that sell complementary products. You'll learn how to forge partnerships in Chapter 4.

- **Calling lists:** Sorting through lists of potential customers generated from online information and visitors to your corporate website. You'll learn how to make these lists useful in Chapter 5.

Please note that you may not need to use *all* these methods in order to get plenty of sales leads. In fact, you may be able to build your entire career just on referrals. However, you should become familiar with all four methods, so you'll *always* have a way to get good sales leads and have plenty of customers.

Remember: The focus on this part is simply building up a list of hot leads. While you might have a brief conversation with a lead (like when you meet at a conference), you are *not* going to sell to them. Not yet.

In Part Two, you'll learn exactly how to contact the leads that you've identified, confirm that they're really potential customers, and start the sales process.

But for now, let's just get you plenty of good leads.

CHAPTER 1

HOW TO WRITE AN EFFECTIVE SALES MESSAGE

Every sales message is a story. Unfortunately, it's usually the wrong one.

Every good story has a hero, a goal, and supporting characters. In lousy sales messages, your firm is the hero, the goal is making a sale, and the customer is a supporting character who either helps or hinders that sale.

In effective sales messages, the customer is the hero, the goal is what the customer wants to accomplish, and your firm is a supporting character who helps that customer achieve that goal.

In other words, when you're writing your sales message, don't try to be the hero who conquers the dragon. Instead, try to be the wizard who gives the hero the magic sword, so that the hero can conquer the dragon.

For example, IBM has an extremely strong sales message, forged through over a century of success. If it were like most firms, that message would be all about how IBM is the largest IT employer in the world, generates more profit than any other technology company, holds more patents than any other U.S. company, etc. But that story, as impressive as it is, is fairly meaningless to anyone who doesn't work there. I mean, seriously, do *you* really care about IBM as a company? Do you really care about a story where IBM is the hero? I know I don't.

But that's not IBM's sales message. The message that IBM's sales pros have been implicitly using since the 1960s is brilliant: "Nobody ever got fired for hiring IBM." That's making the customer into the hero, the smart guy who gets the wizards at IBM working for him.

As any sales professional who has tried to sell against IBM can tell you, IBM's account managers are experts at creating solutions that play into their customer's story line. And they've been able to do that even when IBM was struggling in the market.

HOW TO SAY IT

Here is a sample message that might appear in a sales playbook, along with a rewrite that makes it more effective:

- **Offering:** Online presentation storage and display

- **Current:** "Designonline provides the leading cloud-based software for creating, sharing, and tracking design specifications. With Design-online, engineers can easily transform static content such as schematics and technical documents into voice-enriched design presentations that can be accessed anytime, on-demand."

- **Why it doesn't work:** It's focused entirely on the product and what it does, rather than why the customer might want to use it.

- **Rewritten:** "Today's engineering groups are often dispersed among different facilities or even located in different countries. By using Design-online, your engineers can communicate more easily, anywhere and anytime, using both the written and spoken word. As a result, the typical engineering team can create designs 25 percent faster than using traditional email and file sharing."

- **Why this is better:** It focuses on what the customer wants to do and why the product would be of benefit.

Use Concrete and Emotional Words

An effective sales message also shares two important characteristics:

- It's concrete rather than abstract.

- It's emotional rather than intellectual.

A good way to illustrate this is to use a quote from *outside* of the business world. In your opinion, which of the two quotes below is more persuasive?

- **Quote 1:** "Government action should immediately be taken to end the separation of the German state."

- **Quote 2:** "Mr. Gorbachev: Tear down this wall!"

The first quote is like the typical marketing-written sales message. It's full of jargon, indirect, and wordy. The second quote (an actual quote from President Ronald Reagan) is clearly more effective because it is concrete. It refers to a specific individual, a specific wall, and a specific action, all of which are representative of the central point being made.

The second message is also more effective because it contains emotional color. It uses a verb with emergency overtones ("tear down") and is phased in the imperative mood (as an order or request), which adds dramatic urgency.

Think of messages as having two sliding scales. The first scale has "Intellectual" at one end, and "Emotional" at the other. The second scale has

"Abstract" at one end, and "Concrete" at the other. The most unpersuasive messages are always intellectual and abstract; the most persuasive messages are emotional and concrete. This can be shown as a graph:

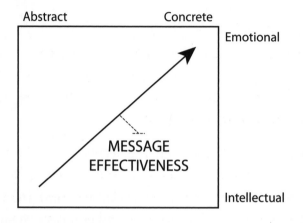

The way to make your sales messages more concrete and give them more emotional color is to rewrite them until they communicate more vividly.

HOW TO SAY IT

Original: It will make your team more productive.
(This is abstract and intellectual.)

Better: Your team will close twice as many sales.
(The result—twice as many sales—is more concrete, but the content is still colorless.)

Best: Your team will celebrate twice as many wins as the other teams.
(This is concrete. It is also emotional through the use of vivid terminology—"celebrate" and "wins." It also surfaces the possibility of winning a competition, which is always an effective emotional spur.)

Unfortunately, most sales messages tend to be both intellectual and abstract, usually through the overuse of business jargon. If there's an attempt at emotional content, it's usually expressed in an abstract way that leeches all the juice out of it.

HOW TO SAY IT

Once again, here are two real-life examples, with rewrites:

- **Offering:** Software designed to help nonprofit organizations manage and produce fund-raising events

- **Current:** "Putting on a fund-raising auction is hard work, and it's easier if you can spread the work out efficiently among your volunteers. Our web-based software lets your volunteers work from home. Since we also let you use your own credit-card processor on the night of the event, and don't charge any transaction fees, you'll also keep more of the money you raise."

- **Why it doesn't work:** Takes too long to say what it says and includes too much detail about features, which are not yet relevant to a potential customer. Also uses vague words like "efficiently." (Compared to what?)

- **Rewritten:** "When holding a fund-raiser, you need every volunteer effort to count. With our software, your volunteers can plan and manage your event, right from their own homes and offices."

- **Why this is better:** Immediately ties to the emotional pressure of putting on fund-raisers, where there's always too much work to do. It also avoids vague words in favor of clear, easily understood phrases.

Reduce Jargon to a Minimum

Jargon consists of technical terms that are useful for communicating inside a company but which can be unintelligible outside the company, or when communicating with customers who aren't "in the know." Because of this, your sales message will be more effective if it uses commonly understood words rather than technical terminology.

HOW TO SAY IT

- **Offering:** Software to track management coaching activities

- **Current:** "Placed in the hands of managers, ACME Coaching Software (ACS) supports all current processes that are already in place to ensure Coaching consistency and that follow-ups are executed. The tool provides upper management the ability to analyze the coaching efforts and correlate impact on performance. Comprised of Coaching, Recruitment, Action Planning, Customer Satisfaction Surveys, and Evaluation tools, the ACS offers a turnkey performance development platform for small businesses and multinational enterprises alike. Building high-performance companies requires effective coaching and activity management. ACS is designed to support managers in targeting, planning, tracking, evaluating, and encouraging employee performance. ACS combines 20 years of activity management expertise with the latest in web-based and portable technology."

- **Why it doesn't work:** It's awkward, wordy, and full of stupid technical jargon and biz-blab.

- **Rewritten:** "The quickest way to improve employee morale and performance is to turn managers into better coaches. ACME Coaching Software helps your managers learn better coaching skills, track the effects of their coaching, and evaluate their own coaching performance."

- **Why this is better:** It's shorter, stripped of jargon, and uses mostly concrete words to explain what the customer would use the product to do.

Edit Out the Buzzwords

A buzzword is any of the dozens of catchphrases that pop up in business conversations. People use buzzwords in order to make something boring seem interesting and impressive. For example, here's an excerpt from an actual business discussion:

> The CIO is a key resource for successful organizations. There is an evolution of roles that happens over a period of time. Organizations haven't even woken up to the idea that there is a critical knowledge chain within their enterprise. CIO roles are not data-processing roles or software application or network management roles or even a clustering of these roles. There is a lot of work going on in shaping the information ecosystem through enterprise architecture and information governance platforms.

That sounds impressive but in fact it's mostly a load of verbal deadweight. Here's a translation of some of the buzzwords:

- "shaping a key resource" = "hiring people and buying them equipment"

- "evolution of roles" = "training and organizing"

- "critical knowledge chain" = "sharing data"

- "clustering of these roles" = "assigning responsibilities"

- "shaping the information ecosystem" = "executing an IT strategy"

- "enterprise architecture" = "an IT strategy"

- "information governance platforms" = "an IT strategy"

So, then, here's what that passage says, in plain English:

The CIO's role is to hire and train people, buy them equipment, and organize them so that they can help other people share information.

Admittedly that sounds a lot less dramatic, but it's also much more understandable and, frankly, more accurate.

When buzzwords sneak into sales messages, it becomes more difficult for listeners to understand what's being said. Worse, it can make the speaker (that would be you) sound like he can't organize his thoughts without sounding pompous or silly.

HOW TO SAY IT

- **Offering:** An operational planning methodology

- **Current:** "Most organizations face real challenges in reconciling corporate intent with operational execution. Delays in execution equal loss. Loss of a sale, loss of good people, loss of market position, etc. We propose using a seemingly simple tool, an org chart, to bridge the gap. The effectiveness of the idea lies in its simplicity and approachability. Everyone knows how to use an org chart. Simple but not simplistic. OrgEnt is a powerful tool that gives you deep and immediate visibility into your entire organization and allows you to model the financial results of potential changes in real time."

- **Why it doesn't work:** The cluster of buzzwords ("operational execution," "market position," "approachability," "deep and immediate visibility," "in real time") obscures the purpose of the offering.

- **Rewritten:** "You put a lot of time and effort into structuring your company. Why not use your org chart to help manage it more efficiently? OrgEnt lets you examine and tune your company's operations in a way that's natural—according to the responsibilities of your entire management team."

Differentiate Yourself

Here's a real-life email I recently received from an executive at a software company. I asked him to position his product. Here's what he sent me:

- You have to move to our software because it'll blow your productivity through the roof.

- If you don't move to our software, your competition will, and they will blow you away.

- Our software is easy to adopt and will make your sales organization more productive.

This executive was convinced that he'd made a compelling case for his software and even thought that the use of words like "blow you away" would create excitement. But, in fact, there's nothing there that would differentiate his company from any other software firm, since they all promise to make you more productive.

Ideally, your sales message should contain at least one solid fact or verifiable statement that separates what you do from what your competitors do.

HOW TO SAY IT

- **Offering:** Management consulting and training

- **Current:** "Whether you're working with individuals, teams, or organizations, we'll work with you to understand what is working, what is not, and create practical solutions that work. Even the best training can begin to fade with time so we provide strategies to keep those learnings alive such as leadership coaching, e-tips, and follow-up surveys. It also means that if you already have leadership models or practices, you don't have to throw them out and start over."

- **Why it doesn't work:** It's not at all clear what's being offered and how it's different from what other training companies offer. As a result, there's little or no reason for the customer to be interested.

- **Rewritten:** "Are your training programs *really* working for you? We aren't a training firm, so we can analyze and measure the impact and return on investment (ROI) of your current programs and ensure that they are fulfilling your expectations."

- **Why it's better:** This message makes it clear what's being offered is unique.

In the examples above, the original sales messages all shared the following characteristics:

- They were about the vendor and/or the vendor's offering.

- They all assumed that the customer would understand why they'd want the offering.

- They were full of either jargon or biz-blab or both.

Business customers don't care about any of that. Business customers care about their own problems, their own goals, and their own customers. Therefore, an effective sales message is always about the customer.

Edit and Hone the Message

Now that you've had some examples, it's time to work on your own message. While there are many ways to write a good sales message, I'm going to teach you the most simple and reliable. This process takes five steps and about twenty minutes.

- **Step 1:** Get into the customer's shoes (metaphorically, not literally). Look at what your offering provides from the viewpoint of a typical customer. How does he see the problem that your offering solves?

- **Step 2:** Start with the phrase "Our customers hire us to . . ." and then write down what your offering does for the customer. That's your first sentence.

- **Step 3:** Start with the phrase "What's unique about our approach is . . ." and then write down something that's different than your competition.

- **Step 4:** Go through the two sentences and examine every word and phrase for jargon and biz-blab. To do this, ask: "What does this mean, really?" If your mind comes up with a simpler phrase, use that one.

- **Step 5:** Examine the remaining words to see if you can make the nouns and verbs more emotional and add a concrete example.

- **Step 6:** Shorten and smooth.

Here's an example:

Original: *Our sales technology solution enables companies to create more productive sales teams by allowing them to track and analyze opportunities through the sales cycle. We do this through use of a customizable analytical engine that generates pop-over fields.*

- **Step 1:** Question: What does the customer really want? Answer: to increase the number of deals that they close.

- **Step 2:** "Our customers hire us to help them increase the number of deals that they close, by making better use of their customer data."

- **Step 3:** "What's unique about our approach is that we have pop-over fields that analyze the data automatically."

- **Step 4:** Replace unique passage with "What is unique about our approach is that you can find out what's going on in a sales opportunity simply by moving your mouse cursor over it."

- **Step 5:** Change "analyze opportunities through the sales cycle" to "find out what's going on in a sales opportunity" and change "pop-over fields" to "moving your mouse cursor over it."

Draft: *"Our customers hire us to help them increase the number of deals that they close by making better use of their customer data. What is unique about our approach is that you can find out what's likely to happen in a sales opportunity simply by moving your mouse cursor over it, and then take action based upon what's discovered."*

- **Step 6:** Shorten and smooth.

Final: *"Our customers increase the number of closed deals through better use of their customer data. They can find out what's likely to happen in any sales opportunity simply by moving a mouse cursor over it, and then decide, based on the results, exactly what to do next."*

Voilà! A perfectly usable sales message.

BUZZWORDS TO AVOID

accountability

actionable

actualize

address the issue

all-hands meeting

alpha office

alternative

analysis paralysis

analytics

aspiration statement

back-end

backward-compatible

ballpark

bandwidth

benchmark(ing)

best of breed

best practice

big picture

bleeding edge

blue-sky thinking

boilerplate

bottom line

brick-and-mortar

center of excellence

champion (used as a verb)

client-centric

closure

commoditize

componentize

conceptualize

co-opetition

core competence

critical path

cross-platform

customer-centric

customer-focused

cutting-edge

drill down

ecosystem

empower(ment)

enable(r)

end-to-end

enterprise-wide

excellence

exponential(ly)

facilitate

fast-track

flattening

flexible

framework

front-end

globalize

goal-oriented

going forward

granular

grow revenues

grow the business

high-level

holistic

impact (used as a verb)

incentivize

industry-leading

infrastructure

integrated

key (adjective)

knowledge base

knowledge management

leadership

leading-edge

leverage

market segment

mind-set

mindshare

mission critical

mission statement

monetize

negative growth

new economy

next generation

next level

nimble

offline

offshoring

operationalize

opportunity (when used as a
    euphemism for "problem")

optimization

out-of-the-box

outside the box

outstanding

paradigm

partner (used as a verb)

performance-based

power shift

principle-centered

prioritize

proactive

process review

productize

proprietary

ramp up

reach out

reality check

recontextualize

reengineer(ing)

regroup

repurpose

result(s)-driven

rich media

rightshoring

rightsize

risk effect

risk management

robust

scalable

sea change

seamless

secret sauce

siloed

skill set

smartsize

solutionary

solutioning

soup to nuts

stand-alone

state-of-the-art

strategic fit

strategic gap

streamline

stretch the envelope

sustainability

synergy

tail risk

talking points

task force

think outside the box

third generation

timely (especially "on a timely basis")

tip of the iceberg

touch base

transition (when used as a verb)

turnkey solution

ubiquitous

user-centric

utilize

validate

value-add

value chain

value proposition

vertical integration

visibility

vision statement

win-win

world class

Where to Go from Here

I occasionally rewrite sales messages for free, as long as I can write about the results. If you email me with your best attempt at a sales message, I might be able to critique it and (at worst) point you in the right direction. You can reach me through www.geoffreyjames.com.

CHAPTER 2

HOW TO GET SALES LEADS THROUGH REFERRALS

A referral is a sales lead that comes from somebody you know. That person might be a customer, or it might be somebody whom you've met in a different business situation or even in a social context.

A referral takes place when a person connects one business contact with another in the hope that they will both benefit. So referrals have nothing to do with being nice. A referral means that somebody is willing to tap into his relationship with someone else by giving them to you. Therefore, when customers refer friends or business contacts to you, they are trusting you to deliver top-notch products and services.

That's important, because that trust "rubs off" on you. Referrals are more effective than other lead generation methodologies because the referrer is eliminating the key uncertainties that block a sale in the early stages, such as "Can this person be trusted?" and "Is speaking with this person worth my time?" Because of this, selling to sales leads generated by referrals is generally easier than selling to sales leads generated by other methods.

How do you get a referral? Put simply, you must ask. And the easiest people to ask are people who already know you and trust you: your friends and colleagues, according to Joanne Black, author of *No More Cold Calling* (Business Plus, 2006).

I interviewed Joanne a few years ago on the subject of referrals and have since had the opportunity to hone my own skills and have spoken extensively with sales professionals who have built up their customer bases in this manner. This chapter is the result of that process.

Referrals from Friends and Colleagues

Sit down in a quiet place and list everyone you know who trusts you. Include friends, family, and colleagues. When you've built your list, rate those contacts according to the following scales:

HOW MUCH DOES THIS PERSON TRUST ME?

    1 = Completely

    2 = Somewhat

HOW LIKELY IS IT THAT THIS PERSON KNOWS A POTENTIAL CUSTOMER?

    1 = Definitely

    2 = Probably

    3 = Maybe

Add up the total of each rating for each individual. The lower the number, the more likely it is that you'll get a good referral from that person. These are the people whom you'll call first. Continue calling until you get all the way through the list.

When you get through to each person, you needn't worry about selling, because this is essentially a social call. You're asking the person to introduce you, based on a relationship that you already have. So, after you've "caught up" on the news, you might say something such as the conversation below.

HOW TO SAY IT

> **You:** Hey, I've started selling supply management systems for Acme. Do you know any manufacturing engineers or managers who work with complex supply chains? I sure could use some help building up my contacts.

At this point, the person you're calling will probably ask you about your new job or what you're doing. Your response is . . . your sales message. Yes, even though you are not actively selling to that individual, your sales message is the crystallization of what you'll be saying to whomever you get referred to.

If your colleague hears a solid sales message that makes sense, you're much more likely to get a referral, because your colleague will know that you've really thought this out and won't make a fool of yourself if they send somebody to you.

Don't Just Ask for Contact Info

Assuming your colleague agrees to help, do not settle for just getting contact information. If all you get is contact information, you're weakening the power of the referral. While you can always say something like "Joe told me to contact you," such phrases are used so frequently that they're meaningless. For all the contact knows, Joe might have given you his name simply to get rid of you! (Don't laugh; it's done all the time.)

You want your colleague to take some specific action that brings you together with the prospect. Rather than asking for a name and number, ask the referrer to call and explain who you are and why you are worth having a conversation with. Ask the referrer to get back to you to confirm that the call has been made or send an email (and copy you on the email).

HOW TO SAY IT

> **You:** It would be great if you could email him and suggest that he get in contact with me. But give me his email address anyway, in case he forgets.
>
> **You:** Do you think that, if I set up a conference call, you could introduce me to her? You wouldn't have to stay on the line, just make the introduction, and then I'll take over.

Follow-Up with the Colleague

Every time you get a referral, you must follow up with the referrer at least three times:

1. One day after the referrer gave you the referral, contact the referrer and express your gratitude for giving you the referral. This is not only polite and appropriate, it allows you to gracefully remind the referrer of the commitment to make the referral.

2. Immediately after you have contacted the person to whom you were referred, send another thank-you email to the referrer and give a status report on the relationship. (For example, "You were right; Fred is a really interesting guy.")

3. If the referral does result in a sale, let the referrer know what happened, and say thank you again. It may also be a good idea to send a small gift of thanks.

Follow-up is essential because you want to gradually "train" your friends and colleagues to send you business. They're more likely to do that if they know that you're grateful and that you obviously value their help.

Referrals from Existing Customers

Getting a referral from a customer is exactly like getting one from a friend or colleague, except that it requires more from you. A colleague already knows you're trustworthy. You'll need to prove to the customer that you're trustworthy, before you get the referral.

Unfortunately, sales pros often ask *brand-new customers* for referrals, right when the first sale is closed. Such requests seldom, if ever, result in sales opportunities because the sales pro has not earned the customer's trust and thus has not earned the right to ask for a referral.

At the point of sale, the customer has shown a willingness to do business with you, but that's all. The customer is already taking a risk by buying from you. Why compound that risk by recommending you to friends and contacts?

Best case, asking for a referral at the point of sale will make the customer feel awkward. Worst case, the customer will think you're greedy and just looking to move on to the next deal. And if you call a day or two later to follow up on the referral request, you'll ruin what's left of the relationship.

There is a way to ask a new customer for a referral, but it involves setting up to ask in the future rather than at the point of sale.

HOW TO SAY IT

Customer: Okay, we'll buy.

Salesperson: Great! I'm looking forward to working with you. We're going to perform for you so phenomenally that you're going to be completely amazed and delighted. But here's what I want you to do for me. I want you to be thinking of a few people who you think should be doing business with us, if we are incredible as we say we are. And after I know that you know that we're the absolute best, I'm going to remind you of this request, but before you give me any names, I'm going to bring you a new customer for your own business. Is that fair enough?

What you've done with that statement is made a commitment and gotten a commitment in return. Your end of the commitment is to make sure that you deliver as promised. Exactly how you do this will vary from industry to industry, but there are four general elements:

1. *Provide incredible service.* Be certain that you and your company provide the absolutely highest level of service in your industry. The resulting credibility greatly reduces the risk of doing business with you.

2. *Be proactive about their needs.* Anticipate what they're likely to want and arrange ahead of time to have it taken care of. Example: Lexus will pick up and drop off your car at your office, leaving you a rental in case you need to drive somewhere during the day.

3. *Provide extra value.* Find something that you can do for the customer that's outside of the expected products and services. Example: you might want to send the customer clippings from articles that deal specifically with their career or hobbies.

4. *Become friends with your customers.* Meet them socially, at business networking events, on the golf course, at informal lunches, or anything else that's not strictly business. Customers who are your friends naturally want to put you in touch with their own friends.

Once you build a relationship with the customer and believe you've provided exemplary service, you have earned the right to ask for that referral.

The best way to discover whether you've earned that right is to contact the customer and ask, not for a referral, but for a simple testimonial. You would do this, of course, after you've been working together for a while and have built up some positive history. Tell the customer that you'd like to share his or her opinions and perceptions with prospective customers. If the customer agrees, ask questions that will flush out any problems that might make a referral, well . . . problematical.

HOW TO SAY IT

You: What could we be doing better?

You: What have we done right for you so far?

You: What would it take for you to refer other people to us?

Of course, if the customer launches into a set of complaints, you know that you're not in a position to solicit referrals. In that case, you'd be wasting your time asking for one.

But, chances are, you'll hear a mix of good and bad. Listen carefully to their responses and write down any comments that might prove valuable in the future. But also look for the series of "green light" answers that indicate that you've built up enough trust that it's fair to request those referrals that you discussed when you closed the initial deal.

You can think of referrals as your sales "report card." The number of referrals that you get—and their quality—tell you how well you are doing at building business relationships and friendships with your customers. If you aren't getting any referrals, you're doing a poor to mediocre job. If you find it easy to get lots of referrals, you're doing a great job.

HOW TO SAY IT

You: [Smiling] So, who are you thinking of referring to us?

You: Have you thought of anyone else who might need our services?

You: I'd love to know whether you know somebody who might be interested in what I've got to sell.

At this point, the customer is now part of your personal network, and you handle the situation identically as if you were asking a friend or colleague. Get the customer to make the call or send the email, and be sure to follow up with the referrer three times.

Where to Go from Here

This chapter is based largely upon my own experience getting referrals and conversations with salespeople who've used it effectively to build business. It also draws upon an interview with Joanne Black, who can be reached at www .nomorecoldcalling.com. Her excellent book is *No More Cold Calling: The Breakthrough System That Will Leave Your Competition in the Dust* (Business Plus, 2006).

Another good resource for referral selling is Jeff Gitomer, who can be reached through www.buygitomer.com. His book is the classic *The Sales Bible: The Ultimate Sales Resource* (J. Wiley, revised edition, 2003).

CHAPTER 3

HOW TO GET SALES LEADS THROUGH NETWORKING

After referrals, the best leads (meaning the ones that are most likely to convert into customers) come from meeting people at industry conferences or other places where decision makers gather, such as charity events, sponsored sporting events, and so forth.

To develop leads in these situations, you need an elevator pitch. Unfortunately, what most people think about when they hear the term "elevator pitch" is a short sales pitch. That's exactly the wrong way to think about it.

The original idea of an elevator pitch was that it was something that you might actually say to a hot prospect who ended up on the same elevator with you. Imagine what you'd actually think if some stranger got into an elevator with you and launched into a sales pitch. You'd think he was out of his mind and get out of that elevator as quickly as possible.

A real elevator pitch is not a sales pitch, but a conversational technique that you can use in social situations to assess whether somebody you've just met is a potential customer. If so, the conversation converts that person into a sales lead, with some kind of contact information.

Make no mistake about it. Chance conversations can definitely result in business opportunities. I personally have made hundreds of thousands of dollars based on contacts I've made at conferences.

Even nonbusiness social occasions are potential lead-generation tools. Bob Carr, the CEO of Heartland Payment Systems (one of the largest credit card processors in the United States) once told me how he sold the idea for his new business to a business contact he met at a wedding.

This chapter teaches you how to have a normal conversation that presents you and your offering in a casual, socially acceptable manner. It builds on the sales message that you created in Chapter 1, but is not exactly the same, because it has to be delivered in a more casual and social setting.

According to sales guru Barry Rhein, an elevator pitch consists of four elements, in this specific order:

1. *The lead-in.* This is the setup statement for the conversation. It's intended to spark initial interest from the (potential) prospect.

2. *The differentiator.* This identifies the sales rep, the sales rep's firm, or the firm's offering as a unique resource that deserves immediate attention.

3. *The engagement question.* This is an open-ended conversation starter that allows the sales rep to assess the prospect's interest level.

4. *The call to action.* This is the request for a meeting to discuss the matter further, thereby moving the opportunity into your pipeline.

Barry explained this approach to me in an interview. What I've done in this chapter is take Barry's basic structure and transform it into more of a conversational tool.

I debuted this conversational version of the elevator pitch on the *Sales*

Machine blog in 2009. The reader response was enormous, and I got many comments from sales professionals who credited it with increasing their ability to use networking events to develop leads.

I'll take you through each of the four parts, in order.

Part 1: The Lead-In

The lead-in is your socially acceptable response to the common question "What do you do for a living?"

When confronted with that question, you can of course say something like "I'm in sales," in which case the conversation is probably over. Or you can say something like "I sell Acme Widgets," in which case the conversation is definitely over. Or you can launch into a sales pitch, in which case you have just made yourself into a nuisance.

There is a better way.

Before your next chance meeting, take a few minutes and compose a sentence that's your best response to the "What do you do for a living?" question. It should have the following characteristics:

- **It must tell a story about your customers.** It explains what your customers do, and how you help them do it better. Note: Tell about your customers, not about you or your firm.

- **The story must be important to a prospect.** No matter how compelling the story, if the dragon being slain (i.e., problem being solved) is actually a tiny serpent, nobody will be impressed.

- **It must contain something quantifiable and defendable.** Your lead-in statement should be backed up with at least one quantifiable fact that proves its validity. This is important because it makes the story real.

- **It must be memorable enough to spark a conversation.** The lead-in should compel the prospect to ask something like: "How in heaven's name do you accomplish [whatever you just claimed]?"

- **It must be short and sweet.** We're talking no more than two sentences, if that. And it has to use real words that actually mean something, not business jargon and catchphrases.

If you're observant, you've probably noticed that this is a conversational variation of the sales message you wrote in Chapter 1. That's intentional. In fact, you'll be using that sales message multiple times and in multiple situations.

HOW TO SAY IT

As an experiment, I asked the readers of the *Sales Machine* blog to send me their conversational lead-ins. I then rewrote them to have more of the characteristics that are described above. Here are some examples:

Original: "Our clients are able to reduce the complexity, costs, and time involved in delivering information, communications, and training into their retail stores."

- **Why it's ineffective:** It is redundant because "complexity, costs, and time" are all varieties of the same thing, as are "information, communications, and training." There are no specific financial benefits. In addition, the sentence is in the passive voice, making it unclear how the seller's firm is specifically involved.

- **Improved:** "Retail firms use our software and services to help train their employees, resulting in an average 10 percent increase in sales, compared to the performance of other stores."

- **Why it's more effective:** It identifies the target market, explains what the seller's firm does, and then provides a quantitative gauge so that the listener can assess the importance of the service.

Original: "Our customers get enterprise quality talent management software at a fraction of the cost to automate employee accountability to achieve results, keep track of employee data, and write performance reviews in half the time."

- **Why it's ineffective:** It's full of terminology that's either vague (e.g., "enterprise quality," "fraction of the cost") or undefined (e.g., "talent management software," "automate employee accountability"). There's no specific, concrete financial benefit.

- **Improved:** "Our customers achieve a 10 to 1 ROI within one year by using our consulting services and software to more precisely focus and track employee behavior."

- **Why it's more effective:** It provides a quantifiable benefit and then explains exactly what the seller's offering does to achieve that benefit.

Original: "I'm a Corporate Account Manager and I work with companies to see if it is possible to help them lower their cost of IT procurement through a business relationship with ___. We have a working relationship with IBM/Lenovo/HP/Apple/Cisco/Adobe and Microsoft to name a few."

- **Why it's ineffective:** Too wordy, and doesn't have a quantifiable benefit. Also it's focused on the seller and the seller's role, which is not as important as the impact that the seller's offering will have.

- **Improved:** "We help companies lower IT procurement costs—typically by 20 percent or more—by negotiating directly with major IT vendors."

- **Why it's more effective:** It gets right to the point and explains exactly what the seller's firm does and the effect it has on the buyer's business.

Original: "We are a provider of online courses for academia, associations, and corporations. We are also a PMI REP and have developed self-paced project management courses such as PMP Test Prep and PM for IT."

- **Why it's ineffective:** This is way too technical. Unless you're already part of that industry and know the jargon, it just sounds like gibberish.

- **Improved:** "Companies like [former customer] and colleges like [former customer] use our online course to get their folk certified as project managers in half the time (and half the money) it usually takes."

- **Why it's more effective:** The jargon has been removed in favor of a quick description of what's being offered and why it's of value.

Original: "We are a 'one stop' human resource consulting and outsourcing firm that provides access to HR services for the continuum of the employment life cycle: recruiting and professional placement; benefits and compensation design; compliance services; organization development; leadership training and coaching."

- **Why it's ineffective:** This is just a string of business terms that have no real meaning. Yes, the listener has a vague idea of what's being offered, but it's all vague and confused. It assumes that all of this "stuff" has some value, an assumption that a prospect might not share.

- **Improved:** "We help our clients with hiring, compensation, compliance, and training, typically saving $**** per employee—a savings that goes straight to the bottom line."

- **Why it's more effective:** This version gets quickly to the business point. The service saves money because it's more effective than the do-it-yourself method.

Original: "We specialize in helping organizations create products and services that wow their markets and then transform their business to deliver those to a predefined cost, quality, service and functional specification—every time."

- **Why it's ineffective:** This is a perfect example of letting the fancy marketing talk get in the way of a good story. The term "wow their markets" is truly cringe-worthy, and the trailing "every time" is probably an exaggeration (i.e., a lie).

- **Improved:** "Companies call us when they want help figuring out what products their customers really want. For instance, we recently helped [former customer] with their launch of [product], which broke all sales records in less than two months!"

- **Why it's more effective:** The abstract nonsense in the original is replaced with a precise definition of what's actually offered and what it can do, based on a prior example. More importantly, it doesn't sound like marketing newspeak.

When you deliver your lead-in aloud, the true test of its effectiveness is whether it sounds conversational. You should be able to say it not just with a straight face, but with enthusiasm, as if you are truly excited about what you do, but without sounding like you're champing to give a sales pitch.

Practice delivering your final version until it sounds natural and casual. Remember, it's the response to "What do you do for a living?" in a conversational, casual situation. So say it at a normal speed and with a smile.

Part 2: The Differentiator

Once you've delivered your lead-in, look at the person to whom you're speaking. Notice whether or not the listener is actually interested in what you said. If all you get is a polite nod, a quick "that's nice," or a shifty-eyed look for the nearest exit, just drop it. The listener isn't a prospect. Let the conversation move on to the weather or whatever else is socially appropriate.

However, if you get a green light to continue, you may have a prospect, so it makes sense to move to the next step. What you're looking for is anything along the lines of "How do you do that?" Ideally, you want to hear that very question (which is what the lead-in is supposed to elicit), but you might get a visual cue (like an interested look) or some other verbal cue (like "Wow!") that signals that it's okay to continue.

Once you get that go-ahead, answer the (implicit or explicit) question "How do you do that?" in a way that positions you and your firm against the competition. The idea is to make it perfectly clear that YOU and your firm are a unique resource that's worthy of the attention.

A "differentiator" should consist of one or two facts. Why only one or two? Most people can only hold—at most—three thoughts in their short-term memory at one time. You've already asked the person to stick your lead-in into short-term memory. Therefore, you only have two (at most) "memory slots" available.

Here's how you come up with a solid differentiator:

1. List as many things as you can that describe how your firm is better (or different) than your competitors.

2. Go through that list and select the two differences that are most likely to be important to a prospect.

3. Write a succinct summary of those two differences in one sentence. Make certain that your summary is free of biz-blab and has a quantifiable benefit.

> **You:** We help our clients with hiring, compensation, compliance, and training, typically saving $**** per employee—a savings that goes straight to the bottom line. (lead-in)
>
> **Prospect:** How do you do that?
>
> **You:** We have a unique methodology and supporting software based on some proprietary scientific research that we funded through MIT. (differentiator)
>
> **You (continuing):** We help companies lower IT procurement costs— typically by 20 percent or more—by negotiating directly with major IT vendors. (lead-in)
>
> **Prospect:** That sounds interesting.
>
> **You:** It is! We've got extensive contacts that let us know the biggest discounts that the IT vendors have offered in the past and use them as the basis for negotiating your price! (differentiator)
>
> **You (continuing):** Our customers achieve a 10 to 1 ROI within one year by using our consulting services and software to more precisely focus and track employee behavior. (lead-in)
>
> **Prospect:** 10 to 1? No way!
>
> **You:** Way! In fact, some of our customers have achieved that ROI in less than six months; and we've got the metrics to prove it. (differentiator)

Part 3: The Engagement Question

In most cases, you'll have already winnowed out the uninterested ones with the lead-in, but it's still worthwhile to check in and be certain that the listener remains interested. The next step is to move the conversation forward so you can set up for a more substantive discussion. You do this with an engagement question.

Engagement questions always start with a conversational bridge, followed by an open-ended question intended to open the conversation to input from the listener.

HOW TO SAY IT

- "Just out of curiosity, what priorities might you have in these areas?"

- "You seem intrigued. Of what I just said, what might be of interest?"

- "Hey, enough about me. How does your firm handle that kind of problem?"

There's no need to get fancy. The most important thing is to make the engagement question conversational. It must sound like something a real person would say to another real person rather than something a sales rep would say to a prospect.

It's particularly important that the engagement questions be open-ended rather than something that can be answered with a simple yes-or-no answer.

HOW NOT TO SAY IT

- "Might your company be interested in our services?"

- "Do you need something like that in your firm?"

That kind of closed-end question simply ends the conversation if it's a NO (even though it may actually be a YES in disguise once the listener learns more). And even if the answer is YES it creates a pause in the conversation, forcing you to ask the open-ended question that you should have asked in the first place. For example:

You: Might your company be interested in our services?
Prospect: Yes.

You: Uh . . . how so?

Prospect: Well, we need that kind of thing.

Awkward. By contrast, an open-ended question keeps the conversation moving.

HOW TO SAY IT

You: Just out of curiosity, what priorities might you have in these areas?

Prospect: We're working with a vendor but they haven't been able to help.

In other words, an open-ended question makes it more likely that you'll learn something useful about the prospect. Hopefully, the ensuing conversation will allow you to prequalify the prospect so you know whether it makes sense to continue the pitch. You may also end up gathering information that will prove useful later in the sales cycle.

More importantly, the ensuing conversation helps build this casual relationship to the point where it's socially acceptable for you to ask for a "real" sales meeting to discuss the matter further.

Part 4: The Call to Action

The point of the elevator pitch is, of course, to generate a potential opportunity. And for that to happen you need to get an appointment for a follow-up meeting. The way you do this varies according to your assessment of the prospect's interest level.

HOW TO SAY IT

SCENARIO 1: *Prospect seems skeptical.*

You: If we really could do (something of value to the customer here), what would your thoughts be on having an initial conversation with us to hear more?

SCENARIO 2: *Prospect seems neutral.*

You: What would your thoughts be on having an initial conversation with us about (something of value to the customer here)? What is your availability over the next few weeks?

SCENARIO 3: *Prospect seems obliging.*

You: I would love to have an initial phone conversation with you about (something of value to the customer here). What is the best way to get on your calendar?

SCENARIO 4: *Prospect is clearly interested.*

You: How do I get on your calendar, please?

The trick here is being realistic about the prospect's level of interest. The more accurately you assess this, the more likely it is that you'll get on the prospect's calendar.

Well, you're almost done, but there's still . . .

Action Item: Rehearse, Rehearse, Rehearse

The great thing about an elevator pitch (as defined in this chapter) is that you only have to memorize about a paragraph. However, the pitch is a conversation—which means that you can't just reel it off like a carnival barker.

For the elevator pitch to work, it must be delivered naturally and conversationally, and, ironically, the only way to be natural is to rehearse until it sounds natural. To do this properly, rehearse with another person who plays the potential prospect and record the conversation. When you play back the conversation, focus on the sound of your voice. You want your words to sound like they're not rehearsed—even though you're rehearsing them! (This is *exactly* what actors do when they rehearse for movie scenes.)

The other thing to listen for is the dreaded "salesman voice." You know what I'm talking about . . . that breezy, TV-pitchman voice that's filled with false excitement. Many real-life sales pros unconsciously talk in "salesman voice" because they've been subliminally cued by years of television and by listening to other sales pros who have it. If you've got "salesman voice"—even the smallest tinge of it—your elevator pitch won't work, because it will sound like a pitch rather than a conversation. Keep practicing until you rid yourself of all traces of "salesman voice," and you'll be ready the next time you meet a potential prospect in a social setting.

More Examples

Here are two samples of complete "elevator pitch" conversations.

> **Person [sitting next to you on plane]:** So, what do you do?
>
> **You:** We help our clients with hiring, compensation, compliance, and training, typically saving $**** per employee—a savings that goes straight to the bottom line.
>
> **Person:** How do you do that?
>
> **You:** We have a unique methodology. Of what I said, what caught your interest?
>
> **Person:** Well, we have about five thousand employees.
>
> **You:** What if it turned out we could save your firm about $5 million per year?
>
> **Person:** [Explains and seems interested.]
>
> **You:** I would love to have an initial phone conversation with you to see whether we can save you some serious money. What is the best way to get on your calendar?

> **Person [met at a technical conference]:** So, you work in IT too, eh?
>
> **You:** Yup. I help companies lower IT procurement costs—typically by 20 percent or more—by negotiating directly with major IT vendors.
>
> **Person:** 20 percent! Off the list price or the discounted price?
>
> **You:** Depends. Tell me a little bit about how you buy XXX today.
>
> **Person:** We buy mostly IBM, right now.
>
> **You:** What if we could greatly reduce your costs?
>
> **Person:** I'd be interested in seeing how much.
>
> **You:** We should talk more. What's the best way to get on your calendar?

A Word About Social Networking

There's a lot of hype surrounding social networking services like LinkedIn, Facebook, and Plaxo. In my experience, the contacts inside them are of limited value because it's so easy to add "friends" and "colleagues" and it's a bit of a contest to see who can get the biggest number of such contacts.

Put simply, there are friends, and there are "social network friends" and the two are very different animals. A friend is somebody who will always take your call. A "social network friend" is usually just somebody who wanted to get on a list.

This doesn't mean that social networking services are not useful tools for B2B selling. They're *extremely* useful for finding out about prospects on whom you might be calling, because they often present a job history. However, social networking just isn't the same as going to a conference and actually meeting people face to face. Yes, it's more efficient, but it's not going to give you the kind of fast track in converting a lead to a prospect that you get with a real referral or a real networking contact.

Where to Go from Here

If you're interested in honing your elevator pitch, or learning all about loading up a pipeline, I can't recommend anyone more highly than the master himself, Barry Rhein. You can get in touch with him through www.barryrhein .com. He teaches lots of seminars, and they're open to individuals as well as companies.

CHAPTER 4

HOW TO GET SALES LEADS THROUGH PARTNERSHIPS

A sales partnership is a semiformal alliance between two or more sales reps to share leads and develop new opportunities. To many sales reps, the entire concept seems a little strange. After all, the traditional view of the sales rep is the "lone wolf" or the "road warrior" who overcomes objections and wins the deal. However, there are two reasons why sales partnerships are a good way to acquire and qualify hot leads.

First, having a partner gives you another set of "feet on the street." Your partner may be calling upon customers who you don't know personally, or who you don't even know exist. For example, suppose you're selling an inventory control system. The need for an inventory control system often becomes painfully obvious once a company begins tracking sales. Therefore, you'd be wise to partner with a rep who sells customer relationships management (CRM) software in your territory.

Second, you'll probably run into some opportunities that can't be developed without help from another rep selling a complementary product. For example, suppose you're selling printing services, and hear about a medium-sized company that needs to produce some glossy brochures and manuals, but can't without the services of a professional graphics art firm. In this case, you might be able to go into the account with the sales rep from a design services firm and, with her, put together a package that would solve that customer's problem.

Sales partners can be one of your best sources of sales leads, if you're willing to take the time to cultivate them and nourish them. Unfortunately, not every sales professional knows how to build the kind of sales partnerships that allow teams of reps to pursue and win these complex opportunities. Effective sales partnerships require the ability to find the right kind of partner and, just as importantly, set the ground rules for working with them. That's what this chapter is all about.

This chapter comes from three sources: (1) experiences of my own from back when I was in high-tech marketing, (2) experiences that sales professionals have shared with me through the blog, and (3) a truly enlightening interview that I conducted with Ed Rigsbee, author of the incredibly useful book *Developing Strategic Alliances* (Crisp Learning, 2000).

Before you can consider a sales partnership, you must understand what you and your firm are bringing to the table. For example, if your company has a strong set of products but little experience selling to a specific industry, you may need to partner with a firm that has few products but lots of experience inside a specific industry. Similarly, if your company is heavily deployed in one geographical region, you may want to develop a partnership with a rep who works in another geographical region in order to develop a global opportunity.

Where do you meet partners? Simple: you'll run into them at the same events that you attended in order to network with potential customers. They'll be at those events because they're interested in the same customers . . . which means that you already have something in common.

There's also a certain level of self-assessment that's required at this point.

It's a natural tendency for individuals to want to keep control of their destiny. As such, many reps feel uncomfortable giving up a certain amount of control over a customer account, which is always part of a partnership arrangement.

Similarly, when it comes to selling, the undeniable fact that "knowledge is power" leads many a rep to hoard information that, if shared with a team, might result in a quicker sale.

Trust needs to be at the foundation of every successful long-term sales partnership. Unfortunately, many sales reps, while trained to develop a certain type of relationship with customers, are often at a loss when it comes to partnering with their peers, particularly when those peers are also (in a certain sense) their competitors.

Select Compatible Partners

If you're going to partner, you need to understand the strengths and weaknesses of your potential partner(s), not just in terms of their ability to contribute to the sales process, but also their willingness (and readiness) to partner. Just because another has a core competency that you need, there is no guarantee that they will willingly share it.

Find partners with whom you can create mutually beneficial value. To do this, look for complementary core competencies and mutual circles of interest. Here is a list of the sort of complementary talents you should be looking for in a sales partner:

- Ability to find opportunities for you in customer accounts.

- Assistance in reducing your overall sales cost.

- Elimination or reduction of duplicate efforts.

- Innovations discovered with their help.

- Access to new customer and prospects.

- Help against established and emerging competitors.

How do you find these things? Some of it is intuitive, but much of the choosing comes from knowing your market and your customers, who they talk to, and where the customer would like to see their suppliers and vendors working together.

For example, suppose you're selling raw computer power as a service that's accessed across the Internet to medium-sized businesses. A natural partner might be a vendor of communications and networking equipment that would need to be in place to make it practical for those customers to use your service.

Another natural partner might be a software vendor that has an application that helps medium-sized businesses to grow. In order to sell her product, that vendor needs to make certain that the customer has the computer power to run it, which is where you come in.

Similarly, suppose you're selling high-powered air-conditioning to light industry located in a rural area of Alabama. A natural partner might be a firm that sells welding equipment that creates heat and smoke that needs to be dissipated in order to increase worker safety.

Sharing a common customer, however, is not enough. You also need to understand why, and under what conditions, it would make sense to partner. There are two sides to this equation: what you expect to get from the relationship, and what the partner expects to get.

Presumably, if you've identified a potential partner, you know the kind of sales leads that you believe that partner can produce, based on the contacts that he's made and customers he's worked with. At the same time, though, you need to know what the partner will expect from you.

The best way to do this is to ask. Find out what they consider valuable. Ask how you can help. The last thing you want is a situation where one partner delivers "value" that the other partner did not consider worthwhile.

During your discussion, hash out a working agreement of who is going to do what and when. Build a plan of action to address the opportunity, spreading the work appropriately among the partners who will be contributing (and benefiting) from the successful sale.

Formalize your agreement by writing down an outline describing the commitment that each partner has made. Include detailed explanations of activities, expectations, and responsibilities of each partner in order to create a road map for your successful alliance. However, be aware that this is only a starting place. It will be necessary to make regular "relationship bank deposits" of physical and emotional energy to keep the partnership alive.

HOW TO SAY IT

EXAMPLE OF A SALES PARTNERSHIP AGREEMENT

- When either party is speaking with prospects, she'll check to see whether the prospect might be a prospect for the other party's offering.

- If it looks like the deal can be expanded to include both our offerings, we'll work together to set up a meeting with the prospect to discuss the matter and to qualify the opportunity.

- Once inside the account, whoever originally developed the account will be the "account manager" and the primary contact. Whoever was called in will provide assistance as necessary.

- All communications from the prospect will be shared between both parties. No meetings or detailed communications will take place without the consent of the primary contact.

- In the event that the prospect's priorities allow for the purchase of one offering, but not another, we agree to share the commission generated by the actual sale.

If the partnership involves ongoing sales activities, both parties should have a frank discussion to reveal potential problems, the nature of the relationship, the scope of the cooperation, and the logistics of the partnering effort.

Any partnership between competing reps is likely to be fragile until the individuals involved learn to trust. The only way to guarantee that trust will grow is to make sure you *always* deliver exactly what you say you will deliver—and then a little more.

Once you get the agreement in place, use it to create leads. The best way to start is to share some of your leads with your partner. Taking the first step will show that you're serious. When doing this, don't just hand them a contact name, like you would a referral. Since this is a partnership, personally and actively bring the partner into one of your accounts and provide introductions to people whom you believe the partner can help. Once you've done this, it's reasonable to expect your partner to reciprocate.

The goal, however, goes beyond sharing leads. Ultimately, you want to build a relationship that allows the two of you to develop brand-new opportunities that otherwise it would be difficult for you to develop alone. In other words, the partnership is about creating new business for both of you, so that you both benefit.

Monitor and Measure

As with any other business situation, great results require ongoing measurement and management. Be sure to consistently communicate to your partner(s) the value you've delivered. Ineffective communication is the primary reason partnerships and alliances fail.

You want to have enough communication so that both parties can monitor the relationship at the "macro" and "micro" levels. Then, when challenges pop up, you can quickly work together to address them. Here are some rules to help you keep the partnership on track:

- Be the kind of partner with whom you'd like to partner. This is the sales partnering version of the "golden rule."

- Ethics and morals are vitally important. Remember: it's not enough to be honest; you've got to avoid the appearance of dishonesty.

- Respect others, their beliefs, customs, and policies. Every company has a slightly different corporate culture; don't assume that yours is better or smarter.

- Think as a member of both your alliance and your industry. As Ben Franklin once said: "We must all hang together or assuredly we shall all hang separately."

- When in doubt, don't! You'll probably run across opportunities where you can use the partnership against your partner. That's like cheating in a marriage. Don't do it.

If the partnership develops problems, don't give in to anger or frustration. Meet your partner more than halfway. If there's money on the table, dispose of it fairly or offer to buy your partner out. Above all, avoid taking the matter to court. The end result of such court cases is pennies on the dollar for you (if you're lucky) and a fat stack of cash for the lawyers.

Getting your partnership from initial handshake to a done customer deal requires plenty of "emotional" fuel. The partners will need to allocate and expend resources, time, mindshare, and energy to turn the opportunity into a sale. As the sales cycle progresses, you'll need to invest in building and strengthening the relationship and the level of rapport.

Don't forget that when the sale is won, celebrate—and make sure that the celebration includes appropriate compensation for everyone involved.

Where to Go from Here

If you're interested in partnership selling, I can't recommend anybody more highly than Ed Rigsbee. I interviewed him a few years ago and he heavily influenced the way I think about this interesting way to sell. Ed is an excellent public speaker, with lots of good ideas to hone your ability to partner. He can be reached at www.rigsbee.com.

CHAPTER 5

HOW TO GET SALES LEADS FROM THE INTERNET

If you're new to B2B selling and have a limited business network, many of the methods described in previous chapters won't work for you. If that's the case, you can begin to cultivate sales leads from the Internet.

At the time of this writing, Internet-based "lead generation" software is in a state of rapid marketing growth, with a multitude of tools and capabilities being introduced every month. In addition, the companies involved in this technology are merging and being acquired by larger firms. Because of that, it wouldn't be meaningful for me to make recommendations, because there's no guarantee that the tools I talk about will be in existence (at least under that name) by the time this book is published.

However, while the tools and firms providing them may change, the generic capabilities don't. Fortunately, that level of understanding is good enough for this discussion because what's important isn't HOW you get the leads, but what you do with them when you get them.

There are two general methods for getting sales leads from the Internet.

The first method is to access an online service that harvests information from the Internet, and then presents you with individuals and companies who might be interested in your offering based on the kind of lead you want to see.

For example, as of this writing, a site for creating lists of possible leads is www.zoominfo.com, which encourages people to share their contact data. When you share your own business contacts on the Zoominfo database, you get access to everyone else's contact data, which at this point consists of approximately fifty million individuals.

As I was writing this chapter, I clicked over to Zoominfo and entered the term "sales manager" along with my local zip code. It produced a list of seven names, which wasn't bad, considering that I live in a very small town.

Currently, Zoominfo offers basic contact information for free, but also sells additional search capabilities and information for an add-on fee. (This combination of free basic use and paid extended use is fairly common for products of this type.)

Some of the other companies that provide contact data harvested from the web are:

- www.salesgenie.com

- www.hoovers.com

- www.leads.com

- www.zapdata.com

- www.infousa.com

- www.goleads.com

- www.lead411.com

- www.linkedin.com

- www.ileads.com

Some of these online services can provide incredibly detailed information about the companies and individuals to whom you might want to sell, including news about their own business situations, additional contacts within the company, people whom your target contact might know, and so forth.

However, the disadvantage of lists compiled from these services is that you have no idea whether the people listed will actually be interested in your offering. You'll be calling them from scratch, and that's much harder than getting through to somebody to whom you've been introduced.

The second method for getting leads from the Internet is to set up a website that harvests the contact information of people who visit it to gather information. Although it's often possible to identify website visitors based on the information that their computer passes through the Internet, it's usually considered wiser to only contact people who've indicated that they wish to be contacted, perhaps by requesting information in return for, say, their email address.

Once your website has that email address, it's often possible to retrieve all kinds of information about that individual, simply based on the ownership of that address. More importantly, websites can be implemented to track the movement of each user through the site, thereby revealing what interested each individual user. That data is stored and compiled and available for viewing when it comes time to actually contact that person.

One of the best ways to find out what's going on in the world of sales technology is to get plugged into the Sales 2.0 Conference, which is conducted under the auspices of *Selling Power* magazine. They tend to feature real-life success stories (which are much more interesting and informative than vendor presentations), but are well attended by the vendors, who often have a variety of marketing, sales, and technical people on hand to answer questions. *Selling Power* magazine itself is also an excellent resource.

The entire subject area of sales technology is fodder for a shelf full of books. However, as I pointed out above, what's important here isn't *how* you get your list of leads, but what you do with them once you have your list.

Regardless of where you get the list of leads, its usefulness will depend on how well you can identify a lead that's likely to "convert" (i.e., turn into a prospect and then into a customer). The goal of this chapter is to help you winnow out the bad leads from the good ones, so you end up spending time "chasing Brinks trucks, rather than garbage trucks" (as the saying goes).

Leads, Qualified Leads, and Hot Leads

There are three levels of sales leads, each of which is more select than the level below.

At the bottom are *undifferentiated leads*—these are essentially names that have been pulled out of a phone book, an industry association list, or any other undifferentiated source of contact information. Among those undifferentiated leads will be some *qualified leads.* These are leads that are potential customers. Among these qualified leads will be the *hot leads*—these will be easiest for you, personally, to close.

The more effort you spend defining what constitutes a hot lead, the easier it will be to recognize them when you see them. However, to discover which leads are "hot," you must first define what constitutes a qualified lead. Here's how:

1. *Define your target industries.* There is a natural set of industries which are most likely to need your product. Winnow down your target industries to the ones that have money to spend and are likely to spend it on your product or services. The result should be one or two industries. If the number is greater than that, continue to eliminate industries until you get down to less than three.

2. *Define your target job titles.* For any product there is a natural buyer who is most likely to make a purchasing decision. Winnow down your

target job titles to those that have the ability to purchase (or greatly influence purchase) your product or service. The result should be one to three job titles. If the number is greater than that, continue to eliminate job titles until you get down to less than four.

3. *Define your target geography.* In many cases, you'll have already been assigned a territory. However, within that territory there may be areas where prospects are more likely to buy your offering than others. For instance, if a competitor has a large facility in one area, that area is generally less desirable, since they'll likely have the inside track.

4. *Define your target "trigger" events.* Trigger events are circumstances that make it more likely that a customer will buy from you. For example, if you sell management consulting, a trigger event might be an announcement of a management change. Similarly, if you sell supply chain software, a trigger event might be the announcement of a merger.

Here are some common trigger events that might create a need for a B2B product or service:

- Acquisition of a major new customer.

- Hiring of a new manager or executive.

- Departure of a new manager or executive.

- Announcement of a layoff.

- Announcement of an expansion.

- Announcement of a move of corporate headquarters.

- Launch of a new product line.

- Retirement of an existing product line.

- Acquiring another company.

- Being acquired by another company.

- Announcement of a new round of financing.

- A move from private to public ownership.

- A move from public to private ownership.

- Announcement of a restructuring.

- Opening of a new factory or facility.

These four factors define the profile of a lead who might become a customer. When you've built this profile, you know now what constitutes a qualified lead. However, if you want to sell more effectively, you need to customize even further and define what makes up a "hot lead."

For example, suppose you're selling an inventory control system and have a pre-customized solution for electronics manufacturing. That's your target industry. You know from experience that the key decision maker when it comes to managing inventory is the VP of manufacturing. That's your target job title.

You've been assigned the Northern New England territory, so your target geography will consist of Burlington, Vermont; Portland, Maine; and Nashua and Manchester, New Hampshire, since these are the cities in your region where you'd be most likely to find any electronics assembly.

The trigger events that are most likely to create an "opening" for a new inventory control product are the announcement of a new product line, a merger with another manufacturing firm, the acquisition of a huge new customer, or a change in management (i.e., a new VP of manufacturing).

Define a Hot Lead—for You!

A hot lead is one that is not just qualified, but also easy for *you* to close—not your sales manager and not the guy at the next desk. To create your own lead scoring metric, you'll need to make some judgment calls about what's really important to you when it comes to closing deals.

Note: If you're in the beginning stages of your B2B sales career, you might not have a precise answer to all of these questions. However, answer them as best you can and then revisit your metric after you've been selling for a few months.

To build your personalized lead scoring metric, answer the following four questions according to this scale:

2 = Very important
1 = Somewhat important
0 = Unimportant

____ **When you're selling, how important is the target industry?** (Example: if you've got a background in a particular target industry, then it may be important to you.)

____ **When you're selling, how important is the job title?** (Example: if you've got experience selling at a particular level, then it may be important to you.)

____ **When you're selling, how important is the geography?** (Example: if your selling style is strongest in a face-to-face meeting, you need nearby prospects.)

____ **When you're selling, how important is a trigger event?** (Example: if you've got specific experience helping firms with mergers, a merger might be important.)

Make a note of your answers, because those numbers will determine which leads you'll contact first, and which you'll put on the back burner or let slide.

Whenever you get a sales lead, use this quick method to "score" it to see whether or not it's going to be easy for you to sell to that lead.

First, ignore any lead that is (1) outside your target market, (2) outside your target job title, or (3) outside your target geography. No matter how "tasty" such a lead seems, you're probably not going to make the sale.

If the lead survives the first check, do a quick online search on the trigger event(s) that are important to your offering. Do a quick scan of the first page of results.

For example, if you sell supply chain management software, you would probably be looking for announcements of new product lines or the opening of new manufacturing facilities. Note in your list (next to the lead) the triggers that you found.

Now, go through the leads that you have not crossed out. Based on your scores from the previous section, fill out the following form:

____ Enter your priority score for the industry.

____ Enter your priority score for the job title.

____ Enter your priority score for the geography.

____ Enter your priority score for each trigger.

____ Have you personally sold to this prospect in the past? (3 for yes, 0 for no.)

For each lead, total the above. The higher the rating for each lead, the "hotter" the lead, and the easier it will be for you to close that lead. You now have a prioritized list of the leads to contact, starting with the ones that are the "hottest."

To show how this works, we'll build on the "inventory control" example that we used previously. Let's suppose that your personalized scoring metric is as follows:

- Target industry = 1. Your background is in sales and inventory control in several industries.

- Target job title = 2. You've got a history of selling effectively to mid-level management.

- Target geography = 0. Your "territory" is purely for convenience; if you got a customer outside of it, nobody would care.

- Trigger event = 1. Your product can improve any situation, so there's demand even in situations that are fairly static.

You turn on your computer on Tuesday morning and discover that three individuals got on your website earlier that morning and both downloaded a white paper about inventory control. You access your online service to retrieve more information about each individual and the companies for which they work. You discover that:

Lead 1 is a technical consultant for an electronics firm located in Nashua, New Hampshire, that was just acquired by a midsized competitor located in Boston.

Lead 2 is a VP of manufacturing in a tool and die firm located in upstate New York. There are no trigger events.

Lead 3 is a CEO who heads a printing firm in Colorado. You used to sell them office automation systems in a previous job. They just won a huge government contract.

Here's how you score them:

	Target Industry	Job Title	Geography	Trigger	Prior Experience
Lead 1	1	0	0	1	0
Lead 2	0	1	0	0	0
Lead 3	0	0	0	1	3

Based on the above, your calling order should be Lead 3 (4 points), followed by Lead 1 (2 points), followed by Lead 2 (1 point).

Refine Your Model

Over the next few weeks and months, keep track of how your sales opportunities are proceeding. While the exact conversion rate will vary from industry to industry, your goal is to get to around one customer out of every ten leads, or better.

If you're not hitting that conversion rate, you need to refine your model. If you're not achieving acceptable conversion rates, you need to find out why. Here's how. Meet, formally or informally, with some of the prospects who didn't buy from you and find out why they didn't. Chances are they'll tell you why you're not making more sales.

In almost all cases, it will be either that you're selling to the wrong people or you're selling to them the wrong way. If it's the former, fine-tune your target market even further. If it's the latter, work to bolster the sales skills in which you are weak.

Many firms wrongly believe that the way to increase sales is to "turn on the spigot" and put more leads into the pipeline, thereby creating more prospects and therefore more customers. But that's stupid, because if your conversion rate is thirty to one and it takes you a week to work through thirty leads, it doesn't matter if there are thousands in the pipeline. You're still only going to get one sale.

If you improve the quality of your leads so that you can achieve a conversion rate of ten to one, you'll make three sales a week, rather than one. You'll also feel much better about yourself. When a sales professional keeps getting no from unqualified leads, it's hard to keep up momentum.

Where to Go from Here

The person who's had the most influence on my thinking on lead generation is Tom Roth, Chief Operating Officer of Wilson Learning Worldwide. I interviewed him several years ago and I've definitely incorporated his thoughts into my ideas on this subject. Roth can be reached through the Wilson website, www.wilsonlearning-americas.com.

How to Fill Your B2B Sales Pipeline

In Part One, you learned to locate sales leads that had the potential to become customers. However, if you're going to sell to them, you still need to contact them (or recontact them, if you met them at a conference) and confirm that they really are potential customers. Your goal for Part Two is to make sure that, when you actually get down to selling (Part Three), you're selling to people who actually need what you're offering, and have the money to purchase it.

Filling the pipeline (aka "prospecting") is hard work because chances are (even if you're selling by referral) that you're going to contact at least some people who are rude, or who resent the fact that you've contacted them. Because of that, in Chapter 6 we'll start by learning an essential sales skill: creating the kind of attitude that's most likely to make you successful in B2B selling.

Once we've dealt with that, we'll move on to initial conversations. Regardless of whether you're calling somebody out of the blue or they're calling you as the result of a referral, you'll need to be articulate about what you've got to offer, and why it's worthy of interest. That's what you'll learn in Chapter 7.

One of the biggest obstacles that B2B sales professionals face is getting through the maze of voicemail that most companies construct around their employees. Chapter 8 explains how to use voicemail to create the conditions where an initial conversation can take place.

Initial conversations, especially cold calling, pose some emotional challenges for many B2B sales pros. Because you'll be starting conversations with people who may not want to talk to you, you're going to encounter a lot of rejection. So in Chapter 9, you'll learn a skill that's absolutely crucial to long-term success in B2B selling—the ability to use rejection and failure as a spur to create greater success.

Once you've gotten into that initial conversation, you need to make sure that the person you're talking to is actually a potential customer. To do that, you'll learn the most important skill for any B2B sales pro: disqualifying sales leads. That's in Chapter 10.

By the end of Part Two, you will have plenty of strong prospects in your pipeline. That's really when the selling begins, which is covered in Part Three.

CHAPTER 6

HOW TO MOTIVATE YOURSELF TO SELL

Until this point, you've been talking to colleagues, going to conferences, chatting with partners, and researching prospects on the Internet. That's easy stuff. Now it starts getting a bit more challenging, because you're going to put yourself on the line to start developing sales opportunities.

The key to being successful in B2B sales is your attitude. B2B selling can be a long process that requires superlative performance, day after day after day. If you're going to be successful at it, you'll need to make optimism, expectancy, and enthusiasm part of your daily experience.

This does not mean being "Little Mary Sunshine" while you're selling. Far from it. B2B selling is a serious business and buyers expect a businesslike demeanor. What I'm talking about is cultivating the inner drive that gives you the energy to do what's necessary to sell at the highest level.

I think you'll find that if you take this chapter seriously, every other element of B2B selling will be easier to accomplish. We're laying groundwork here, so take this chapter seriously, please.

You Are in Control of Your Motivation

One of the biggest lies in the business world is that people are motivated by a combination of the carrot and the stick. The concept assumes that people are like donkeys that will move forward to get the carrot or to avoid being whipped.

What's stupid about that imagery is that donkeys don't behave that way in real life, and neither do people. If a donkey doesn't want to move, it will not move, no matter how hard you hit it. And if a donkey isn't hungry, it's not going to move to get the carrot, either.

People are exactly the same way. The motivation to act doesn't come from the externals of punishments and rewards, but from the way you perceive the world and what you value in it. In other words, *your attitude, your motivation, is* not *the result of what happens in the world, but how you interpret what is happening in the world*.

Take the weather, for example. In the United States, many people feel depressed when it's raining and uplifted when it's sunny. In the Middle East, many people feel the exact opposite—a cooling rain is an excuse to have a picnic under a tree. Similarly, many adults grumble when it snows, while most children are delighted. It's not the weather that creates the mood, it's how the weather is interpreted!

Arguing that "children like snow because they don't have to go to school" is missing the point. A snowbound child could just as easily mope around inside and complain about not being able to play croquet because it's snowing. But children don't do that because they tend to interpret snow as an opportunity to play and are therefore motivated to get suited up and get out to make some snow angels.

The same thing is true in business. A sales rep making a sales call while it's snowing can grouse about the extra drive time or she can look forward to the appreciation that a customer might feel because she is committed enough to fight the weather to make the meeting.

Weather, of course, is just one small element of what one faces when selling, but the same thing is true of other aspects of the business world. Take, for instance, a bad economy.

When the economy goes south, it does become more difficult to sell, because buyers tend to become more conservative. However, there are many sales professionals who do *better* when the economy sours, because they see that tighter budgets mean an opportunity to get buyers to consider new vendors.

What's important here is the understanding that *you* are in control of your attitude about things, and therefore *you* are creating the conditions under which you're most likely to feel motivated. Therefore, if you're going to get motivated and keep motivated, you need to create an optimistic mental filter that views the events in your day-to-day world in a way that gives you energy and enthusiasm.

Neutralize Your Negative Triggers

Your first step to maintaining a consistently positive attitude (and therefore stay motivated to sell) is to stop letting exterior events trigger negative thoughts. This is often hard at first because events that will make it more difficult for you to sell can and will happen. The trick is to not let *your feelings* about those events influence your attitude and motivation making it *even more* difficult to sell.

Suppose you're traveling to a customer meeting but keep running into red lights and traffic delays. As this continues, you realize you're going to be late for the meeting. That IS going to be a problem. However, if you start feeling bad about it, you've got *two* problems: the fact that you're late, and the fact that you're flustered because you're late. This is definitely a "two for one" deal that you can do without.

If you let the delays "mean" that it's an "unlucky" day, there's an excellent chance you're going to walk into the customer meeting feeling depressed and demotivated. The prospect will sense this and may wonder whether you're a naturally moody person. Now you've got a third problem: the customer is focusing on your problem, rather than the other way around!

To get a different result, you must modify your interpretation of exterior events that might trigger your negative outlook. Once events take on a different, more useful meaning, they won't trigger a bad attitude.

For example, while the delays may be making you late, you can use the extra time to collect your thoughts, consider your options, and decide on a damage control strategy. Or you may use the time to come up with a better schedule, so that you always leave plenty of time, just in case there's traffic.

Your feelings about the event will be determined by how you describe the event to yourself. To keep those feelings from creating additional problems, reframe the situation so it has a meaning that will build your positive attitude and continue to keep you motivated.

HOW <u>NOT</u> TO SAY IT

- "This is going to be a bad day."

- "I'm always unlucky."

- "This is all I needed!"

- "!#%%$#& red lights!"

HOW TO SAY IT

- "This could happen to anybody."

- "It's no big deal to be a bit late."

- "Now I have time to rehearse my presentation."

- "I've learned an important lesson about traffic in this town."

Obviously, that's only one example of the kind of setbacks that can take place. No matter how large the setback, there is always the opportunity to turn it into something positive, if only as a signal that you need to make some adjustments in order to be more successful. If you make it your business to learn from every setback and stay focused on your end result, setbacks are simply way stations on the road to success.

Reframing setbacks requires patience and the ability to listen to (and edit) your internal dialogue. However, while it's sometimes difficult, there are few mental activities that will pay dividends more quickly.

Detoxify Your Media Consumption

The media bombards us with highly emotional messages. Overexposure to the news can really kill a positive attitude. Thirty years ago, news programs primarily provided people with information intended to help them understand the issues of the day. Today, however, most news broadcasts consist of "info-tainment" specifically crafted to support commercial messages.

Much of today's news programming consists of "if it bleeds it leads" stories followed by commercials offering some form of security or comfort. The idea is to amp up your fear/anger/frustration and then encourage an action, like buying "comfort food," which promises to relieve the pressure.

This constant flow of negative imagery and commentary can not only destroy a positive attitude, it can actively create a negative attitude about life and the world. If you want to maintain a positive mood, consider reducing, or even eliminating, your exposure to broadcast news programming.

Instead, read the business section, or better yet, spend more time with some motivational tapes, music that raises your spirits, or great literature. Stick to media that help your attitude to constantly improve. In his book *Attitude Is Everything*, Jeff Keller points out that it's easier to achieve and maintain a positive attitude if you have a "library" of positive thoughts in your head that you can draw on if the day doesn't go exactly as you'd prefer.

Starting each day reading, or listening to, something positive helps ensure that you have such a "library" to draw on. Consider reading an inspirational book right after you wake up. You might also want to spend your commute listening to motivational tapes rather than the news.

Along these lines, don't forget that music is a time-honored way to manage your moods and attitudes. Consider investing in music that you find motivating and energizing. Use it to "pump yourself up" right before your big meetings or to cool you down when things get challenging.

Use your imagination to find new ways to pump positive thoughts and feelings into your head. Set a target of at least fifteen minutes a day, but don't limit it to that. The more time you commit to positive media, the more benefit you'll see in your attitude, your motivation, and your consequent sales success.

Avoid Negative People

You probably have one or more friends, relatives, or acquaintances who make you feel tired and drained. They always seem to have something sour to say; criticisms come to their lips far more quickly than compliments. If you tell them of a success that you've had, their congratulations ring hollow. You sense that they'd just as soon have you fail. What a drag (literally)!

Such people are toxic to your attitude (and hence to your success) because, if they're not actively tearing down your enthusiasm, they're trying to get you to think the same way about the world as they do.

If you want to maintain a positive attitude, consider sharply limiting your daily exposure to such people. Don't show up at the daily "watercooler complain-fest." Don't go to lunch with the "grouse and grumble" crowd. If you've got a family member who is constantly negative, tune her out. Life is too short to waste listening to somebody grouse.

It's especially important to avoid people who constantly foist their strong opinions on others. Such people usually have surprisingly negative views about others, especially those who disagree with them. Having a conversation about race with a bigot, for example, is the mental equivalent of taking a bath in raw sewage.

Unfortunately, there are going to be times when you are forced by circumstances to be in close proximity to one of these "Debbie Downers." For example, if you've got a customer who has a chip on his shoulder about some political issue, it may not be possible to avoid a tirade.

The trick here is not to get drawn into lengthy gripe sessions and (above all) not to get sucked into an argument. When you *must* deal with such people, limit your own conversation to the business issues you need to address. When the other person goes off on a tangent, listen respectfully for a while, then change the subject to a more positive topic as soon as possible.

HOW TO SAY IT

- "Wow! I can tell that upsets you. The last thing I want to do is to make things more difficult for you by neglecting a key business issue. I wonder if you could go over these figures with me?"

- "I can't tell you how much I appreciate that you want to share with me your good fortune in finding a belief that's clearly so satisfying to you. I'll certainly think about what you've said, but right now, we'd better get back into figuring out these terms and conditions."

Adopt a Positive Vocabulary

The words that you use—both what you speak aloud and your internal dialogue—have a vast influence in how you perceive what's happening in the world. All words carry a certain amount of emotional baggage, inherent in their exact definition and the way that they've been used in the past.

For instance, the words "despise," "hate," and "dislike" mean essentially the same thing, but carry very different emotional baggage. If you "dislike" something, but tell yourself that you "hate it" over and over and over, it will intensify the original emotion.

In other words, your vocabulary doesn't just reflect what's in your brain; your words also influence the way you think about the world. Negative feelings create negative words, which create more intense negative feelings. Similarly, positive feelings create positive words, which create more intense positive feelings.

One of the best ways to keep a positive attitude, therefore, is to use weak words for negative feelings, and strong words for positive ones. That way, you end up thwarting the downward spiral of negative feelings and words, and accelerating the upward spiral of positive feelings and words.

So stop complaining about things over which you have no control, such as the economy, your company, the customers, etc. And stop griping about your personal problems and illnesses. What does it accomplish, other than to depress you and everyone else?

Expunge negative words from your speech. Substitute neutral words for emotionally loaded ones.

HOW <u>NOT</u> TO SAY IT

You: That pisses me off.
You: I'm totally enraged.
You: !%&!# off, you !@%$#!

HOW TO SAY IT

You: That peeves me.
You: I'm really annoyed.
You: [dignified silence]

Similarly, when describing positive or neutral things, use words that have power and energy. One of the most successful people in the sales world today is Gerhard Gschwandtner, the publisher of *Selling Power* magazine. The word he uses constantly to describe life, the way he feels, and the creative ideas around him is "terrific." Not surprising, "terrific" people are drawn to him.

HOW <u>NOT</u> TO SAY IT
Coworker: How's it going?
You: Hangin' in there. Same old, same old.

HOW TO SAY IT
Coworker: How are you?
You: I feel great! How about you?

Where to Go from Here

There is certainly no lack of motivational speakers and trainers in the world. Some of them are little more than entertainers, but there is one who, in my opinion, has a program that is particularly useful for people in B2B sales: Jeff Keller.

Jeff was kind enough to spend an hour with me, discussing ways to manage your attitude, and thereby create a wellspring of motivation. This chapter is inspired by Jeff's ideas, leavened with some perceptions from other motivational speakers. I've also included some ideas that *Sales Machine* readers have shared with me over the years.

Jeff Keller can be reached through www.attitudeiseverything.com. Jeff's truly excellent book is *Attitude Is Everything: Change Your Attitude . . . and You Change Your Life!* (INTI Publishing & Resource Books, 2007). I can't recommend it highly enough.

CHAPTER 7

HOW TO HAVE INITIAL CONVERSATIONS

An initial conversation is when you speak with a lead for the first time, officially in the context of possibly doing business. If you got that lead through a referral or networking, you've got a leg up, because the lead already knows who you are.

However, even then, you still have to do the same things that you'd do if you simply called a lead out of the blue—you need to find out if they're really a prospect, and not just a lead that eventually won't pan out.

To make the concept easy to understand, I'll assume that you're attempting the most difficult kind of initial conversation—the dreaded cold call. If you can learn how to make an effective cold call, then fielding an initial conversation from a referral or social contact will be relatively easy.

This chapter will lead you through the entire process and show you how to qualify as many prospects as possible. (Note: When you run into voicemail, use the techniques described in Chapter 8 to get to the initial conversation.)

The Fear of Cold Calling

I once ran a poll on the *Sales Machine* blog asking how sales professionals felt about cold calling. Most of them disliked it, only 25 percent liked it, and a measly 4 percent said that it was their favorite sales activity.

Unfortunately, many B2B sales pros tend to see cold calling as either a necessary evil or something to be avoided. In fact, cold calling is so unpopular that there's an entire segment of the sales training industry committed to helping people avoid cold calling.

Why is cold calling so feared? Three reasons.

First, cold calling, by its very nature, means that you're going to be interrupting people who weren't expecting you to call. Since even sales professionals don't enjoy being interrupted in this manner, cold callers are painfully aware that they're doing something that, if looked at the wrong way, is intrusive and obnoxious. And since most sales professionals like to help people and build relationships, they naturally look askance at any situation that forces them to violate social norms.

Second, the recipients of cold calls feel that they have a blank check to treat cold callers with disrespect, anger, irritation, and all sort of emotions. A cold call is an opportunity to vent frustration that might have been building up all day or all week. Unfortunately, rude behavior in this situation is not just tolerated in the business world, but actually encouraged. There are dozens of videos on YouTube, for instance, consisting of recipients of cold calls treating sales professionals shabbily, apparently because people find such behavior amusing.

Third, and most importantly, cold calling generally means "failing" more than "succeeding," if you define "succeeding" as converting a lead into a prospect. (At it turns out, that's not the case, but it's easy to think about it that way.) Nobody likes to fail, and so sales professionals naturally prefer to avoid a situation where they're not constantly winning.

What's ironic about all of this is that cold calling needn't be a horrible chore or involve all sorts of bad feelings about rejection and failure. That's why a quarter of all sales professionals actually like cold calling and some even like it better than other parts of their job. They've learned the secret of doing cold calling the right way and (just as importantly) *thinking* about cold calling the right way.

If you read this chapter carefully, complete all the action items, and adapt the "How to Say It" segments to your own offerings, I think you'll find that cold calling becomes at least tolerable. In fact, you may find that you actually enjoy it.

Prepare Your Script

Now it's time to build a cold calling script that will actually work in a B2B environment. Your cold calling script is a variation of the sales message that you crafted in Chapter 1. However, that script will need to be altered in order to be effective in a cold calling environment. According to cold calling expert Keith Rosen, a cold calling script for B2B sales should:

- Be about thirty seconds long.

- Start with your name and company (no small talk!).

- Request permission for a brief conversation.

- Deliver a specific, compelling reason for the prospect to want to continue the conversation.

- Uncover whether there's a problem in their business that you can help them fix, a need you can fill that they may or may not even be aware of, or an opportunity to deliver additional value.

The goal of the script is to make the lead realize that there is some problem or limitation that is negatively affecting their business and that you might have a solution to that problem. When that happens, the natural response for the lead is to continue the conversation. In that case, you can set a future appointment to explore the possibilities of helping.

HOW TO SAY IT

> **You:** Rick, this is Josh Snider from Ace Delivery. May I take a few seconds to tell you why I am calling and then you can tell me if we should continue speaking?
>
> **Lead:** Okay.
>
> **You:** I work with owners of small manufacturing companies that from time to time are frustrated because their customers do not get their shipments on time as promised, even though you completed the job on time. They are concerned about retaining their customers in the face of more competition and are looking for ways to increase the reliability and consistency of product delivery. Rick, are any of the things I mentioned issues for you or is everything running 100 percent smoothly?

You will know whether the lead is a potential customer based on their response. If they do not have any problems that you can fix, then honor your agreement and politely end the call.

What If the Lead Doesn't Want to Talk?

What if you ask "May I take a few seconds to tell you . . ." and the lead simply says no?

There are two schools of thought on this.

One school says that you terminate the call. You say something like "Thank you for being honest with me" and then hang up.

The other school of thought says that you should phrase the script so that you're still respectful of the lead's time, but still check to see whether a conversation is possible. Here's a script that does that:

HOW TO SAY IT

> **You:** Hi, John. Jim here from Acme Cost Control. Did I catch you at an okay time?
>
> **Lead:** No.
>
> **You:** John, I'm sure you're busy and I want to respect your time, so I'll be brief. The reason for my call is this. We just saved Universal Transport an additional 12 million dollars in shipping costs, so I thought it was important to reach out to you, since every company has an obligation to their customers and shareholders to reduce expenses as much as possible. I don't know if you have a need for our services, but with your permission, let's talk for a few minutes to determine if there is anything we're doing that could benefit you. Would you be comfortable spending just a few minutes with me on the phone right now, if I stick to this timetable?

Under this second school of thought, it doesn't matter whether the lead says yes or no to the conversation, because you're committing to being brief. The danger with this approach is that it can seem pushy.

One of the most popular posts on the *Sales Machine* blog contained a script that followed this second school of thought. Here it is:

HOW TO SAY IT

> **You:** Hello [prospect's first name], this is [your name] from [your company], have I caught you in the middle of something?

In most cases, the prospect will respond one of three ways:

- Response 1: "It's always a bad time, but what's this all about?"

- Response 2: "No, this is not a bad time. What can I do for you?"

- Response 3: "You know, I'm glad you asked because I'm right in the middle of heading out the door. Call me later this afternoon."

If Response 1 or 2, say:

You: I know I'm calling you out of the blue, Joe, but sometimes, if I don't know anyone at the company I'm calling, this is the only way to develop a relationship. All I want to do right now is quickly introduce myself, my firm, and my offering to you. As I mentioned, I'm with [your company] and we help companies [what your company does] and I was wondering how I would best position myself to determine if our product may be a fit for you?

If Response 3, say thanks, and then call back at the time they asked. You'd think this seems obvious, but most cold callers do not do this, but instead just move to the next name on the list. That's dumb, though, because the lead just gave you permission to call, so you're no longer cold-calling. You don't have a prospect (yet), but you're further along than if you just called out of the blue.

When you call back, if you get through to the lead, treat the situation as you would have if you got response 1 or 2. If you end up in the lead's voice-mail, say:

You: Joe, you asked that I call you around this time, but it looks like you're out. Call me at XYZ number, but if I don't hear back from you by this Friday, I'll call you on Tuesday.

Once again, you need to be certain to actually call back when you said you would. When you actually do so, you'll separate yourself from 95 percent of the other sales professionals who are cold-calling. (Note: You might want to use a scheduling program, like the calendar feature of Microsoft Outlook, to keep track of the callbacks that you need to make.)

A Final Check of Your Script

The main thing at this stage is to come up with a short, sweet script that "feels right" and "seems natural" to you. You don't have to worry about getting it perfect though, because you'll have plenty of time to tune and change as you go along. In fact, as you cold-call, you can test different variations to see what works best for you.

Before going any further, call your own voicemail and pretend that you've just gotten a prospect on the line. Go through your script, then listen to a playback. As you listen, answer the following seven questions:

1. Did I communicate respect for the customer's time?

2. Did I sound like I'm focused on helping the customer?

3. Did I obtain permission to continue the conversation?

4. Did I immediately identify who I am?

5. Did I provide a compelling reason to speak with me?

6. Did I mention a customer-oriented benefit?

7. Did I avoid details that would normally emerge later?

If any answers to those questions aren't an emphatic yes, then you need to edit or rewrite your script.

Practice, Practice, Practice

Now that you've got a script that you know will work, rehearse the script until it sounds natural. This can be more difficult than it seems at first glance, because the mind goes through three stages when learning a script:

1. *Reading:* You sound like you're reading something from a piece of paper.

2. *Reciting:* You sound like you're reciting something from memory.

3. *Acting:* You sound as if the words are coming spontaneously from the heart.

If you've ever been to a long-running play, you've probably wondered how people can say the same lines over and over, night after night, and make them seem as fresh as if they were just on the tip of their tongue. That's what rehearsal does. Eventually, the script disappears and becomes part of your thinking. Little variations appear automatically that make it sound more genuine and real.

I recommend rehearsing your script at least two dozen times. Once you've completed your basic rehearsal, you still have to make sure that you're not speaking in the dreaded "salesman voice."

Create a Schedule and Follow It

To be successful at cold calling, you must schedule a regular time each week to make the calls. Rather than setting your schedule to meet your convenience, though, it's wiser to call when your leads are most likely to be converted into real-life prospects.

Dr. James Oldroyd, now a professor at the Sung Kyun Kwan Graduate School of Business, conducted a study of cold calling success in 2007, working with the Kellogg School of Management. The study covered companies of various sizes in over 40 industries, and the cold calls, in this case, were in response to a sales lead accessing a corporate website (a common means of generating a list of undifferentiated leads).

He discovered that much of the conventional wisdom about cold calling was dead wrong. For example, conventional wisdom is that the worst times to call are early in the morning (because the individual will be annoyed at being bothered first thing) and at the end of the day (because the individual will be getting ready to leave). Instead, the best time to call is right after lunch, because the individual will be relaxed and ready to undertake a new task.

It turns out that none of this is true. According to Oldroyd's research, in order to convert a lead to a prospect, the best times to call are between 8 a.m. and 9 a.m. and 4 p.m. and 5 p.m., and the worst time to call is between 1 p.m. and 2 p.m. In fact, 8 a.m. to 9 a.m. is 164 percent better than calling between 1 p.m. and 2 p.m. Please note that is not Oldroyd's opinion; it's a statistical fact based on actual performance, as measured by the systems that track conversion rates.

Why are those times so good? Nobody knows exactly, because Oldroyd's research didn't cover the "why" of it. However, it's pretty easy to speculate as to the reasons behind the statistical phenomenon.

The 8 a.m. to 9 a.m. time is probably effective because decision makers often come in early to get work done and are more likely to answer the phone if called before the official workday starts.

The effectiveness of the 4 p.m. to 5 p.m. time is most likely the result of the fact that fewer meetings are scheduled during that time, because people don't want to stay late. As a result, decision makers are more likely to be in their offices.

Meetings are often scheduled at 1 p.m., and people may be out to lunch between 1 p.m. and 2 p.m., making the leads less likely to be available.

However, this is all guesswork. What's important is the statistical fact, which makes it easier to schedule your cold calling time to be more effective. Knowing the "why" of it may be interesting, but it's not going to win you any customers.

There are also myths floating around about what day is the best to call. Some sales professionals swear by Monday, since that's when everybody is setting their agendas for the week, while others swear by Friday, since that's when people are more likely to be receptive and flexible (as in "casual Friday").

Both viewpoints are wrong. Oldroyd's research indicates that the best day to call is Thursday and the absolute worst day to call is Friday. Oldroyd's research also revealed the extremely valuable fact that sales leads generated from websites have a very short useful life. With such leads, the best time to call is within five minutes from the time that the lead was viewing your website.

In fact, you are four times more likely to successfully qualify a lead if you call within five minutes than if you call between five and ten minutes, and you are twenty-one times more likely to qualify a lead if you call within five minutes than if you wait for thirty minutes.

What this tells you is that regardless of the time that you schedule your cold calls, you should give the highest priority to hot leads that access your website during the hours that you're cold-calling. Jump on those leads quickly, because they are the most likely to convert into prospects.

Your success with initial conversations will depend not on your product or the quality of your leads, but on your attitude as you approach the cold calling process. Here is where Chapter 6 of this book is invaluable. If you've been following the prescriptions in that chapter, you'll have no problem getting yourself motivated to call during the time you've scheduled.

Beyond that, there are four things that you should do right before you start calling, that will "lock down" your attitude so you're as effective as possible at your job:

1. *Use a headset, not a handset.* You want both hands free so that you can talk as if you're talking in person.

2. *Sit up straight and smile.* If you're slumped and frowning, the prospect will "sense" it, even from a distance.

3. *Visualize success.* Think of a time when you won a big sale. Put your mind and memory and emotions in that place.

4. *Lay aside your sales goals.* These get in the way if you focus too much on them. It's about the customer, not about you.

You are now ready to make your calls.

A Word About Gatekeepers

You've probably noticed that all of the techniques above assume that you'll actually get through to the person whom you're trying to reach. That, however, isn't always going to be the case. A lot of the time, you'll end up in voicemail. If so, don't despair, because in Chapter 8, I'll explain how to use voicemail to qualify a lead into a prospect and potentially move the sale forward.

Sometimes, however, you're going to run into gatekeepers, whose job is to protect the person you're trying to reach from, well, you. If so, rejoice. In today's lean and mean corporate world, the only people who have human gatekeepers are real decision makers.

How, then, to get through the gate? There are essentially two approaches, depending on the level of the gatekeeper.

If the gatekeeper is a receptionist, you simply bypass. The easiest way to do this is to tell the receptionist to put you through to Accounts Receivable.

Companies always want to get paid. Because of this, there is *always* somebody answering the phone personally for Accounts Receivable. Furthermore, that person usually isn't trained as a gatekeeper. Here's how to do it.

HOW TO SAY IT

Receptionist: Acme Industries. May I help you?

You: Accounts Receivable, please.

Receptionist: Right away, sir!

Ring, ring.

Accountant: Accounts Receivable.

You: Gosh! I'm sorry. I'm trying to get through to Jane Bigwig. Do you have her extension?

Accountant: Uh, okay. It's 1776.

You: [Writing it down] Could you do me a favor and ring me through?

Ring, ring.

Decision maker: [Looks at caller ID and wonders why Accounts Receivable is calling her] Yes, what's going on.

You: [Script]

Even if you don't get connected, you now have the decision maker's direct dial, so you can call repeatedly until you get her on the line.

If that feels too manipulative, then your best bet is to ask the receptionist to connect you to the decision maker's admin. The admin, of course, is just another gatekeeper, but it's a gatekeeper who knows exactly how to sell to the decision maker.

Once you've gotten to the admin, use the specter of a well-known competitor to create the impression that your call is important enough to put through, or to schedule a time to talk with the executive.

Admin: Joe Bigwig's office.

You: This is John Doe from Acme Supply Chain. I need to speak to John about how [competitor] is outsourcing their manufacturing.

Admin: He'd probably be interested in that, but he's not available right now.

You: When will he be available for a call?

Where to Go from Here

There are dozens of books and seminars on the subject of cold calling, and dozens of sales trainers who can help you refine your cold calling script, technique, and follow-through. My favorite expert on general cold calling issues is Keith Rosen. He is a genius when it comes to deconstructing the psychology of cold calls from both the seller's and the sales lead's perspective. He can be reached at www.profitbuilders.com. His book (a must-read if you're going to be cold-calling a lot) is *The Complete Idiot's Guide to Cold Calling* (Alpha Books, 2004). (Don't let the title fool you. It's for anyone who's looking to do better, especially if you want to avoid sounding like an idiot when cold-calling.)

Another good source of information is Wendy Weiss, who is the main source of input for the next chapter, which covers prospecting using voicemail. She's smart and one of the nicest people I've met in the sales training world.

Finally, you can't talk about perfecting your cold calling technique without considering Andrea Sittig-Rolf, who gives seminars on the subject all over the world. She can be reached at www.blitzexperience.com, and her most relevant book is *The Seven Keys to Effective Business-to-Business Appointment Setting: Unlock Your Sales Potential* (Thomson/Aspatore Inc., 2006).

CHAPTER 8

HOW TO PROSPECT USING VOICEMAIL

Most sales training programs assume that you'll be involved in either a face-to-face meeting or a phone conversation. While they concede that voicemail is a barrier to one of those two events taking place, the emphasis is on bypassing voicemail rather than using it as a sales tool.

That, frankly, is a bit ridiculous, because many executives and lower level employees screen *all* their calls and only have one-on-one conversations that have been scheduled ahead of time. The reason is simple: they're so overwhelmed by all the communications that go on in the business world that they're using voicemail to create some space and sanity. Good for them, but bad for you.

Not long ago, I thought of voicemail as an unsolvable problem that had to be tolerated. However, I happened to interview cold calling expert Wendy Weiss, who came up with the core of the technique described in this chapter.

After interviewing Wendy, I put a version of her system on the *Sales Machine* blog, where it became an instant hit, and generated lots of comments and additional ideas. This chapter reflects her original input and the comments from people who applied it in real-life selling situations.

Create a Voicemail Script

When most B2B sales pros make a call and end up in a voicemail situation, they tend to do one of the following:

- **Tactic 1: Transfer.** You try to get the call transferred to an admin to find out a better time to call. This used to work, except that nowadays, you're going to end up in the admin's voicemail. The only person answering the phone is the receptionist, and even she's not answering when she's on break or at lunch.

- **Tactic 2: Terminate.** You figure there's no sense leaving a voicemail, so you terminate the call and (sometimes) make a note to call the decision maker back at a later date. Most of the time, however, you end up back in voicemail anyway.

- **Tactic 3: Babble.** Now desperate, you try to leave a message, but because you are not prepared, you babble and then leave a phone number at the end of the message, which you repeated so quickly that it's impossible to understand. Then you wonder why you didn't get a call back.

Well, forget all of that. Think about voicemail as an effective way to start a sales opportunity, and give it the same level of attention that you gave your cold calling routine. First, you need a script.

According to Wendy, a voice message script consists of four parts:

- **Part 1: Identify yourself.** Say your name, your firm, and your telephone number. Be sure to say your name and phone number at the speed you would if dictating to someone who is going to write it down. Your prospect will interpret this slow dictation as a direction to write and pick up a pen and begin to write. If your name is at all difficult, spell it slowly; you want your prospect to be able to write your name down.

- **Part 2: Explain why you're calling.** Write a one-sentence statement about the value, benefits, and outcomes that you, your offering, and your company deliver to your customers. This should include a quantifiable financial impact that's meaningful to the customer.

- **Part 3: Provide proof you can deliver.** Write two brief success stories about a similar company with whom you have worked and how you were able to help them. Keep this short! Three sentences should be enough.

- **Part 4: Identify yourself again.** Say your name, firm, and number again at the end of the message. Slowly. This way, if your prospect missed the number the first time, she won't have to go back to the beginning of the message. Make it easy for your prospect to call you back!

You've probably noticed that all of this is quite similar to your core sales message, your elevator pitch, and your cold calling script. That's intentional. They're all variations of the same thing, and that's why we've been paying so much attention to them.

HOW TO SAY IT

- **Part 1:** Hello! I'm Wile E. Coyote (C–O–Y–O–T–E) from Acme Devices, 8–0–0–5–5–5–1–2–3–4.

- **Part 2:** The reason I'm calling is that our inventory control systems save our clients an average of $1 million in excess costs and I'm curious to know how much money we might be able to save for you.

- **Part 3:**

  - *Version A:* IBM recently hired us to save around $200 million in its part inventory by building a customized solution; I can send you a case study if you're interested.

  - *Version B:* System Builders Unlimited—they're down the street from you—recently credited us with decreasing their customer response time by three days. This resulted in their most profitable quarter.

  - *Version C:* The Widget Manufacturers association recently sponsored a study showing that we had the most efficient solution for controlling inventory inside companies like yours.

- **Part 4:** If this is interesting to you and you think it's worthwhile for us to have a brief conversation, please call me back. I'm Wile E. Coyote (C–O–Y–O–T–E) from Acme Devices, 8–0–0–5–5–5–1–2–3–4. Have a great day!

Rehearse, Rehearse, Rehearse

Give your voicemail script the same attention and love that you gave to your cold calling script. This may be more difficult than you think because you're probably used to leaving casual, unplanned voicemail for friends and colleagues, so you likely have some bad habits to break. In addition, it takes practice to work with a script so it doesn't sound like you're just reading it.

Call your own voicemail and practice leaving messages. As with your cold calling script, don't just read the script but "interpret it" as if it were part of a conversation. Alternate the "part 3" case study. Play with different ways of emphasizing the "part 2" reason that you called.

As you are rehearsing, play back the recording and make sure that you are giving your *entire* name, firm, and number. *Clearly!* That's the most important part, because the more clearly you give that information, the more likely it is that the prospect will write them down. And they're only going to call you back if they write that information down, right?

After you've left yourself about twenty messages, get into your voicemail system and play them back. Notice how you sound. Listen for which statements worked and sounded the most genuine.

If you're not satisfied with how you sound, keep rehearsing until you are.

Create a System So You'll Follow Up

Now that you know what to say, create a system. Selling by voicemail requires persistence and regularity. This isn't because you're going to make yourself a pest. Quite the contrary. It's that consistency that's going to subtly suggest to the lead that you're reliable and trustworthy, which will increase the likelihood of actually winning a personal conversation.

Here's how you do this. Make a call. If you get through to a decision maker, great! Since you've already learned how to successfully cold-call, you already know how to handle that situation.

If (as is likely) you get into voicemail, leave a message, as prescribed earlier. Remember to use *only one version* of the part 3 mini case study.

The likelihood is minimal that a prospect will call you back from only one message. So put a reminder in your calendar to make another call in three to five business days. Note: You might want to use the calendar function in Microsoft Outlook to handle your scheduling.

If the prospect does *not* call you back when those three to five business days pass, leave another message, using a different part 3 mini case study. Once again, schedule another call in three to five business days.

If the prospect *still* does not call you back, when another three to five business days pass, leave yet another message, using the final part 3 mini case study. Once again, schedule another call in three to five business days.

If the prospect *still* does not call you back then you leave what Wendy calls a "Last Chance Message." This message has the same beginning and ending as the previous voicemail messages, but the middle is different.

In this message, you make sure the lead knows that you understand she's busy. Tell her you're assuming that it is not a good time to have a discussion with you, so you will *not* be calling again for a while. Specify a time frame, six months, a year—that way they know you're serious.

IMPORTANT: Make sure you keep an even tone, nothing that could be interpreted as angry or annoyed. Shoot for the normal friendly, businesslike manner you use to communicate with peers. As with the other messages, practice a bit using your own voicemail.

Why does this work? Sometimes the statement that you won't be calling can make an interested (and extremely busy) prospect pick up the telephone and call you back. It helps overcome procrastination if the prospect was intending to call but never got around to it.

As you continue to leave voicemails, be sure to keep track of what's working and what's not. Track the conversion rates of the prospects that call you back. Try different scripts and measure which ones work better. The more effort and precision that you put into measurement, the more effective you'll become at selling in this manner.

Where to Go from Here

The expert here is Wendy Weiss. In addition to being almost frighteningly charming, she's particularly strong when it comes to training women to cold-call. She can be reached through www.wendyweiss.com. Her latest book is *The Sales Winner's Handbook: Essential Scripts and Strategies to Skyrocket Sales Performance* (DFD Publications, 2010).

CHAPTER 9

HOW TO COPE WITH REJECTION WHILE PROSPECTING

A positive attitude can be difficult to maintain in the face of failure. For example, if you lose a string of opportunities, it's hard not to take it personally. If left unchecked, the fear of failure can become a major stumbling block to a career in B2B selling.

Fortunately, it's possible to transform that fear into something useful.

While overcoming the fear of failure is not specific to B2B selling, it is potentially far more devastating than in other types of selling activity. Because B2B selling often involves contact with successful executives, being rejected seems more serious, almost as if you're being denied access to an exclusive club.

In addition, B2B sales opportunities often take months to develop, which means that you may be investing a great deal of time in one opportunity. It can hurt badly if a prospect rejects a proposal that took weeks of your time to write.

I've found that most sales professionals "white knuckle" themselves through failure. At key moments in the sales cycle, they steel themselves for rejection, believing that being prepared will make it hurt less when it happens. Unfortunately, that fear makes it woefully difficult to sell, because it keeps your focus on you and your emotions, when you should be focusing on the prospect.

Rather than enduring the fact of rejection and failure, a better approach is to use it to your advantage. To teach you how to do this, I'm going to draw on what I learned in an interview with bestselling author and motivational speaker Art Mortell. I took what I learned from Art, incorporated it into my own experience, and subsequently posted about half a dozen blog entries discussing my own views on the subject.

The response from the blog readership (which was extensive) was split into two camps: those who "got it" and understood that rejection is only a minor annoyance and those who seemed determined to cling to the pain.

I'll leave it to you to decide which of the two groups is most likely to be successful at B2B selling.

In my view, you absolutely *must* conquer your fear of failure if you're going to be successful at anything that involves selling, but particularly in B2B selling where so much is at stake.

Invalid vs. Valid Rejections

In selling, failure is always a kind of rejection, either a rejection of YOU as the individual from whom they want to buy, or a rejection of your offering, as something they want to buy. To expunge the fear of failure, we must first get at the part of the failure that stings the most: the rejection.

According to Mortell, there are two types of rejections: valid and invalid.

Valid rejections are when a person doesn't do what you want them to do because of something that you can change. For the purposes of this discussion, I'll use some really basic examples from cold calling. That's rejection at the beg.

For example:

HOW <u>NOT</u> TO SAY IT

You: Hello, John. How are you doing today? [Wait for response] I'm calling businessmen in your area to see whether you want to take advantage of . . .

Lead: [Hangs up]

That's a valid rejection, because the cold calling script is overly familiar and pushy. A different script might have worked so, in this case, the rejection was valid.

Invalid rejections are when that "failure" took place because of something completely arbitrary that's outside of your control. Here's an example:

HOW TO SAY IT

You: Hi, John. Jim here from Acme Cost Control. Did I catch you at an okay time?

Lead: Why the !#$%! do salespeople keep calling me? Go !#$##@! yourself. [Hangs up]

Clearly, the person you just called has some issues. Anybody who called them would likely get the same response. You could have started with a perfect sales script and you'd still have gotten the same response. It's not about you, so it's not a valid rejection.

This is true even when the reaction of the other person isn't churlish. For example:

HOW TO SAY IT

You: Hi, John. Jim here from Acme Cost Control. Did I catch you at an okay time?

Lead: Are you a salesperson?

You: Yes, and I was hoping to speak with you.

Lead: I never speak directly to salespeople. [Hangs up]

What happened in this case is that you accidentally broke the prospect's rules. You had no way of knowing that the lead had the belief that she shouldn't speak directly to sales professionals. And since you violated that person's rule, it's just a conflict of rules, not a valid rejection. It's just luck.

What's important here is that the prospect's reaction really didn't have anything to do with you personally, because anybody else taking the same action at the same time would have gotten the exact same result. You simply took an action that didn't have the result that you prefer.

Remove the Sting of Rejection

The minute you decide not to "own" invalid rejections, some of the sting of rejection vanishes. However, even invalid rejections can make you feel bad if you get a lot of them in a short amount of time. And there are still those valid rejections to be dealt with . . . times that you tried your best but still got shot down, not because of a conflict of rules, but because you didn't perform to your satisfaction.

The first step to overcoming the fear is understanding why rejection stings. The answer may surprise you.

Do you think you work because you want money? Wrong. What you really want is what the money can buy, and I'm not talking about that new Ferrari. I'm talking about the feeling that owning a Ferrari might give you. No matter what reason you give for being in sales (or indeed any other career), trace it back, and you'll eventually get back to "it makes me feel good about myself."

That's why rejection hurts. There's something about the situation of being rejected that makes you feel bad about yourself. To test this theory, imagine the biggest idiot you've ever known telling you that you're stupid. Do you care? No. The rejection fails to sting because it doesn't assault your sense of self. Who cares what that oaf thinks?

According to Mortell, rejection starts to sting as the result of three subjective factors:

1. *Frequency.* Everyone can deal with *some* rejection, but how much rejection can you experience before you start taking the negative feedback to heart? How many times can you contact a qualified prospect and get a negative response before you begin to take it personally? In other words, getting told a million times that you're stupid might make you question your intelligence, even if you didn't particularly respect the people saying it.

2. *Emotional involvement.* How emotionally involved are you in the person who's doing the rejection? When somebody knows you through conversations and meetings (especially face-to-face meetings), it's easy to assume that their rejection of you is valid since they "know you."

3. *Perceived importance.* As a sales rep, you're likely to feel most comfortable contacting people who are of a similar (or lower) social class or educational background. However, you might find yourself avoiding people whom you feel are more important than yourself, because their rejection of you might seem to carry more weight or authority.

Everybody is influenced by these three factors to varying degrees. Some people can shrug off a long series of cold calling rejections, but feel it deeply if a colleague criticizes their work. Others only feel bad about rejection when it's a top executive doing the rejecting.

What you need to do at this point is get introspective for a moment and determine the circumstances that make you feel bad about being rejected. Understanding why you feel rejected is the first step to removing the sting. To do this, take a different approach, depending on the subjective reason that's behind your feeling of being rejected.

Now that you know why you feel rejected, your job is to weaken the ability of the rejection situation to make you feel bad about it.

1. *Frequency.* To make yourself feel less vulnerable in this area, throw out all the invalid objections. Don't even count them. They're nonsense. If you still feel that you're getting a lot of rejections, then look at the norms for other professionals at your level. If you discover that you're in the ballpark for everyone else, there's no particular reason to feel bad about being rejected. If it turns out that you are getting valid rejections more frequently than your peers, then you'll need to figure out what sales skill is missing or broken in your tool kit, and then work on it.

2. *Emotional involvement.* The cure for this subjective ailment is to focus less on the outcome and more on the process. Once you realize that there is a fair amount of chance involved in many sales situations, you have an emotional attachment to doing your best, rather than an attachment to the achievement of an actual goal. This has the advantage of putting you "in the moment" so that you can perform better.

3. *Perceived importance.* The cure for this is simply to believe in yourself and your importance relative to the people you're contacting. Here's the honest truth: if you're offering something that's crucial to the success or happiness of your customer, you are as important as the biggest bigwig on the planet. Here's another big truth: most bigwigs are exceedingly average people who've stumbled into their success. They're only human, not demigods.

The trick to bulletproofing yourself against rejection is to let people have their own emotions and beliefs, and then simply use whatever happens as either a signal to improve your skills (a valid objection) or a signal to exercise your "so what" mental muscle (an invalid one).

Reframe Failure as a Part of Success

Hopefully by now you've stopped worrying about the invalid rejections, and you're more aware of your rejection foibles and have taken some corrective action. Now it's time to harness rejection to make you more successful.

In sales, the number of rejections you get is directly proportional to how successful you'll become.

It's true. The people who hit the most home runs are the ones who get up to bat the most. As has been pointed out innumerable times, the person with the major league baseball record for being struck out is Reggie Jackson, one of the greatest batters of all time.

I have met dozens of B2B sales professionals who have stories of how long it took them to make a sale and how many times they had to get rejected in order to make their quotas. The simple truth is that if you're not getting rejected, you're not really selling.

The best way to make the connection between rejection and success is to do the math. Suppose you've come to dread cold calling, or calling people inside an account you're developing, because it seems like you're getting rejected all the time.

Estimate the number of times you encounter rejection in an average day. (No need to be entirely accurate; go ballpark here.) Now calculate your daily average salary/commission. Now divide the number of rejections per day by your daily salary. For example:

- Average number of times you get a valid rejection each day: 5

- Your daily salary and commission, on average: $500

- The money you make every time you get rejected: $100

Look at that number carefully. That's how much money goes into your pocket every time you encounter a rejection. The reasoning is simple. If you're not getting rejected, you're not selling. So when you do sell, it's because you've been willing to be rejected. The rejections lead to the sales, so you're being paid to be rejected.

Now take a Post-it note and write down the following equation in big, bold letters:

$$REJECTION = SUCCESS$$

Make two more Post-its. Stick one by your phone. Put one where you see it every time you open your briefcase. Put the third in your bathroom where you'll see it when you get ready for work in the morning.

It sounds a little corny, but the technique works because it forces the equation into your subconscious mind. Leave the Post-its up until they fall off. Then make new ones.

Once you've made that connection, you need to harness the *valid* rejections into what they really are: a signal that you need to spend more time improving your sales skills. Notice where in the sales process you got rejected and see where it went wrong.

For example, if sales leads are "turning off" at the end of your script, figure out why your script is not engaging them to enter into a conversation. Make changes; try different approaches until you find one that works.

Where to Go from Here

In my opinion, the expert on handling failure and rejection and turning it into something positive is motivational speaker Art Mortell. His new book is *How to Enjoy Failure, Be Amused by Rejection and Thrive on Anxiety*, which can be ordered at www.artmortell.com.

CHAPTER 10

HOW TO CONVERT A LEAD INTO A PROSPECT

Until this point, the goal has been to get into a substantive conversation with the sales lead. But what do you do when you're actually in the conversation? Do you start selling? No! Absolutely not!

Once you're in a conversation with a sales lead, your primary job is to *eliminate the lead from your list*. You only want to sell to people who are actually going to buy, so you must figure out quickly whether the lead is "real" or not. And if not, move on.

The bane of every B2B sales pro is the false prospect—a prospect that's never going to become a customer. You can end up spending hours, weeks, and months developing a false prospect, only to discover that you've been chasing a rainbow.

You only want to spend more than a few minutes of time with a prospect if:

- The prospect's firm really needs your offering.

- The prospect's firm has money to purchase your offering.

If neither of those is true, *you are wasting your time*!

Unfortunately, many sales pros are so thrilled simply to be talking to a sales lead that they don't want to burst the happy bubble by finding out if they're really a potential customer. The sales pro assumes that because the lead is willing to speak with them, they must be a potential customer.

Not so. The lead might be willing to have a conversation with you because:

- He feels bored or lonely and just wants to talk to somebody.

- She hopes to have the offering . . . someday in the far future.

- He's looking for a cat's-paw to play against your competitor.

- She's confused about her firm's real needs.

- He wrongly believes that your offering costs a fraction of what it actually costs.

- She's looking for new contacts for a future job hunt.

- He thinks you sound cute and wants to ask you on a date.

Whatever. From your perspective, there's no sense in pursuing the conversation unless there's a real need for your offering, and some money to pay for it.

Find Out If There's a Need

To make sure the prospect's firm really needs your offering, you must find out if the goal or problem that your offering addresses is actually of importance to them. To do this, discuss the prospect's needs during your first conversation, and what you're selling. During this conversation, gracefully introduce questions like:

1. What are some of your priorities right now?

2. What are some of your challenges surrounding your current goals?

3. What problems are you encountering?

4. What would you ideally like to change?

The response will reveal whether the need is great enough that it makes sense to continue.

Let's suppose you're selling a computer application that helps companies reduce excess inventory. You've gotten a referral and are now talking to a person who's interested in what you have to say. The actual questions you'd ask are:

1. What are your priorities when it comes to handling inventory?

2. What are some of the challenges you face while trying to reduce your inventory costs?

3. Ideally, where would you like to be in terms of inventory levels?

4. Tell me about the problems you are encountering in your supply chain.

Any of these questions could easily launch into a discussion of the details about the customer's needs and will prove useful as you position and differentiate your offering.

WARNING: Do not simply ask questions as if you're interviewing a job candidate. The questions need to emerge naturally out of the conversation. For example:

HOW TO SAY IT

You: Tell me about your priorities around your supply chain.

Lead: We have run into problems with accelerated growth and although a good thing, it is causing us some real headaches.

You: What would be some examples of headaches it is causing?

Note that the discussion addresses priorities and challenges. Of course, the curious salesperson would ask more layering and probing questions around the customer's response to really understand the customer's true business problems.

However, if it turns out, during the discussion, that they don't really need what you're selling, politely thank the contact for her time, and withdraw. Any further time put into this "opportunity" is wasted. For example:

HOW TO SAY IT

You: Joe told me that you've got a supply chain problem?

Lead: Very much so. We can't get enough product from our supplier and our customers are driving us crazy asking for more.

You: Why do you think that is?

Lead: Because we only have one supplier.

You: Ah! My company sells complex systems to handle complicated supply chains. I wish I could help, but it sounds like your supply problem isn't our area of expertise. But thanks for speaking with me . . .

Find Out If There's Money to Buy

If it turns out that the prospect does have a need, then you need to find out if they have the money to buy your offering. This is more complicated than it seems, because every company that isn't actively in bankruptcy has money to spend, if they think it's a priority to spend it on something.

Your job is to make sure the customer's firm sees whatever your offering addresses as an important enough issue to justify making the investment. To do this, ask questions that uncover all the impacts of the problem or goal that your offering addresses.

HOW TO SAY IT

You (example 1): What has been the impact of the issue not being addressed?

You (example 2): You mentioned not being able to sell more. What's been the impact of not being able to sell more?

You (example 3): What have been the consequences of this issue?

Remember, don't ask these questions like an interrogator but instead work them into a normal conversation. During this conversation, you'll need to make a judgment call. If it appears that the sales lead has other priorities that are clearly more important than whatever your offering addresses, thank the person politely and withdraw.

If the Lead Is Real, Set Up the Next Step

If you sense that the sales lead has a need and considers it a financial priority to address that need, you're ready to add them into your pipeline as an honest-to-goodness prospect. To do this, ask for the next step. Your next step will usually be a further meeting to discuss the possibility of going forward.

Note that in most cases, you do *not* want to have a substantive discussion during your initial conversation. The point of the initial conversation is simply to confirm that you've got a real prospect. In many cases, you will have interrupted the sales lead, making it a bad time for the more substantive conversation to come.

During the appointment that you've scheduled you'll spend time uncovering more detail about the prospect's problems and goals, and finding out how the decision makers involved would go about purchasing your product. For now, though, you want to make an appointment for a *real* sales call.

This entails asking for a block of the sales lead's time.

HOW TO SAY IT

> **You:** [Pick one that feels right for the conversation.]
>
> . . . What would be your thoughts on having an initial conversation with us about _____?
>
> . . . What is your availability over the next few weeks?
>
> . . . How would I get on your calendar, please, for an initial conversation?
>
> . . . What is the best way to get on your calendar?
>
> . . . How does this week work, or is next week more convenient?

Once you have made an appointment, you are past the prospecting stage. The sales lead is now a real prospect and you are dealing with a real opportunity. In Part Three, you'll learn how to develop the account and move it toward the eventual sale, when you have the substantive discussion that you set up during this lead qualification process.

Where to Go from Here

A great source for honing your qualification skills is Barry Rhein, who can be reached at www.barryrhein.com.

PART THREE

How to Develop a B2B Opportunity

Once you've confirmed that your sales lead is a real prospect, and put that prospect into your pipeline, you have to convince the prospect—and probably some decision makers in the prospect's firm—to actually buy your offering.

Therefore, your next task is to figure out who in the prospect's firm makes the decisions to buy whatever you're selling, and exactly how the prospect's firm would go about buying it. The result of that process is your sales campaign document. I explain how to gather that information in Chapter 11.

Once you've gotten the "lay of the land" and put it into your campaign document, you'll meet with individual decision makers, influencers, and stakeholders, to get their buy-in to the idea of buying your offering. That's the subject of Chapter 12.

As you're working to build consensus, you'll likely be asked to present to groups of decision makers and influencers. In Chapter 13, you'll learn how to give a powerful and compelling sales presentation. You may also be asked to demonstrate your offering. In Chapter 14, you'll learn how to give a demonstration that helps move the sale forward.

If the money involved in the purchase of your offering is significant, or if the issue your offering addresses is vital to the prospect's firm, you may be asked to write a sales proposal, perhaps based on a request for proposal (RFP) document. In Chapter 15, I cover the politics of such documents and how to write them so that they help you sell.

At the end of Part Three, you'll know exactly how to bring your prospect's firm to the point where they'll make a decision. In Part Four, I'll explain how to close the deal, negotiate final terms, and set up a system to constantly improve your ability to sell.

CHAPTER 11

HOW TO DEFINE YOUR B2B SALES CAMPAIGN

When you're selling to a small company (i.e., less than fifty people), it's usually easy to figure out who has the power to make a decision. It's usually the CEO, maybe with the help of a technical expert. As you try to sell to a larger firm, things quickly get more complex.

That's not all. If what you're selling will change the way multiple people within the organization operate (like a new computer system), you can easily run into dozens of people who have a stake in seeing that the right decision is made.

So, since you're certain that this is a real prospect, start laying out your sales campaign. Find out who the players are, and convince your initial contact to help you get meetings with them.

This is far less complicated than it sounds at first glance. In fact, it's one of the easiest steps in the B2B sales process. Here's exactly what you say:

Work the following questions into the conversation:

> How are buying decisions of this kind generally made?
> Who normally controls the budget for this kind of buying decision?
> Who is going to need to be on board for a decision to be made?
> Who can say no to the decision to buy?

If your contact doesn't know the answers to these questions, ask your contact who *would* know, and then ask them to set up a meeting.

Once you've determined who you need to get on board and how the buying decision is going to be made, you're ready for the next step.

Note: You may discover that offerings such as yours are typically purchased through the writing of a proposal. We'll be covering that in Chapter 15.

Document How the Customer Buys

A prospect's needs (and ability to react to those needs) will vary according to what's going on in their business. It's those needs (and the budget) that are driving the pace and timing of the purchase. Your job is to help that buying process along by raising the priority of the purchase, building consensus that a purchase will take place, and insuring that the buying process moves forward.

I interviewed sales funnel expert and business process consultant Mark Sellers on this subject. He explains that B2B customers typically go through six stages when they're purchasing a big-ticket item:

- **Stage 1: Problem recognition.** The prospect's firm is not going to buy anything unless they perceive that they have a problem that needs solving. Note that a problem can also be an opportunity; the inability to address that opportunity represents the problem that needs solving.

- *Your job at this stage:* You'll be working with your initial contact and perhaps one or two decision makers to clarify the details of the problem. (You'll learn how to do this in the next chapter.)

- **Stage 2: Define economic consequences.** The prospect's firm can't possibly make an intelligent decision on whether the problem is worthy of attention until they have an idea of how much the problem is costing them. Without a dollar number attached to it, a problem is just a wish list.

  - *Your job at this stage*: You'll be working with your initial contact, and perhaps one or two decision makers, to generate these estimates. (You'll also learn how to do this in the next chapter.)

- **Stage 3: Commit funding.** If the customer recognizes that there is a problem and that the problem has economic consequences (stages 1 and 2 above), then they'll have to decide if taking the next logical step of committing funding to solve the problem is worth the effort. They may not know the exact amount, but they're willing to put down, in writing, a number that represents an intent to spend.

  - *Your job at this stage:* You'll be presenting your findings about the problem to large groups and speaking one-on-one with decision makers to build consensus that there is a problem and positioning your solution as the most likely way to fix it. (You'll learn how to do sales presentations in Chapter 12.)

- **Stage 4: Define decision criteria.** It is only after the customer has gone through all three stages above that they begin to define how to fix the problem. Previously, they may have had an idea of what's needed (e.g., we need CRM because we're losing customers to the tune of $10 million a year), but they haven't determined how they'll decide which system to buy.

- *Your job at this stage:* You'll be working with the customer on some document, such as a request for proposal (RFP), that defines the problem officially and states how they expect the problem to be fixed. (You'll learn how write proposals in Chapter 13.)

- **Stage 5: Evaluate alternatives.** This is when the customer looks at the available solutions and decides how they will fit with the budget that has been set to fix the problem. Note: If there is no firm commitment on the four previous stages, a sale is probably *not* going to take place.

  - *Your job at this stage:* Continue to present and meet with decision makers to build momentum and to fend off any possible competition. (You'll use skills from Chapters 11–14 to do this.)

- **Stage 6: Select vendor solution.** It is at this point that the real decision is made, based on the commitments made at all five prior stages. Needless to say, if you've worked closely with the customer on the previous five stages, you are almost guaranteed to win the final business because you've helped to "frame" the problem, the budget, and the criteria.

  - *Your job at this stage:* Close the deal and work through the final negotiations. (You'll learn how to do this in Part Four.)

At this point, don't worry about actually *doing* all these stages. All you need to worry about is mapping out the process above and documenting the people who will be involved. This document becomes your guidebook for how you'll approach the account. It also provides a way to record who's who and what's happened, so that you don't get confused if you're handling several different opportunities at the same time. In fact, without a sales campaign document, you'll be limited in the number of opportunities that you can handle, simply because human memory is so fallible.

The sales campaign document also helps you clarify and confirm the customer's buying process. In most cases, you'll want to share this document with your initial contact to confirm that your plan makes sense, and that you'll be pursuing the opportunity in a way that is likely to result in a successful outcome.

HOW TO SAY IT

A typical sales campaign document that you prepare for your own use might look like this:

DESCRIPTION: Microsemi offers a variety of embedded devices, including eight-bit microcontrollers; specialty memory products such as electrically erasable programmable read-only memories; and code-hopping devices used in keyless locks, garage door openers, and smart cards. Its chips are used by tens of thousands of customers in the automotive, computing, consumer, industrial, medical, and networking markets.

REQUIREMENT: Microsemi is experiencing significant quality problems due to their outsourcing of supply chain to rural China. They need a convenient way to accumulate test results on components in order to identify problems before they ripple through the supply chain, creating bad runs at their final assembly plants. Preliminary estimates are that this problem is costing them $2 million a year, roughly 1 percent of their $200 million a year revenue stream.

LIKELY SOLUTION: Our silver-level supply chain report module, along with customizations to make sure that it can draw data from their existing ERP system. Estimated cost is $1 million, which will provide an ROI within six months.

DECISION MAKERS: The following people will need to be fully committed in order for a purchase to take place:

- Terry Moon, VP of Manufacturing—Responsible for the problem and has the most stake in fixing it. He's well regarded in the company, but not seen as a power player, which is why this hasn't been addressed sooner. [phone, email]

- Mikel Kallima, CIO—Holds the budget for all IT purchases. Will need to be brought on board or he can block the sale. [phone, email]

- Will Jorryn, CFO—Insists on signing off on any purchase greater than $500k. [phone, email]

- Brasen Rangle, Director of Supply Chain Logistics—He's my initial contact and source. He reports to Terry. He'll be responsible for training personnel on the new system, so he needs to be in the loop. [phone, email]

- Skip Karsen, Engineer Emeritus—He's the architect of the ERP customization and usually against "foreign" additions to his system. He may present a problem and will need to be won over to this approach. [phone, email]

DECISION-MAKING PROCESS:

- **Stage 1: Problem recognition.** The problem is widely recognized inside the manufacturing group, which has been complaining about it for years. However, top management has been focused on stock growth. I will need to raise the priority of this problem by meeting with Kallima and his team.

- **Stage 2: Define economic consequences.** We will need a confirmation that the estimates are correct. To do this, I'll need to work with Moon, who will be able to set me up with Jorryn in order to confirm the numbers.

- **Stage 3: Commit funding.** At this point, Moon will need to sponsor me to a meeting of the steering committee to present the results of the previous two stages, along with a draft solution. Prior to that, I'll need to set up meetings between Rangle, Skip, and our engineers to confirm feasibility.

- **Stage 4: Define decision criteria.** The company seldom writes official RFPs, so we'll be able to move forward with a letter of intention. This should be joint-authored by Moon, Rangel, Kallima, and Karsen.

- **Stage 5: Evaluate alternatives.** Karsen will probably want to confirm that their current ERP vendor lacks this capability and make certain that there's not a better approach. I'll need to give a presentation to an evaluation team (unclear at this point who will be on the team).

- **Stage 6: Select vendor solution.** Assuming we are the selected vendor, we'll work through the details and move forward with the installation.

PURCHASING PROCESS: Once consensus is reached, Moon will write an official request to Kallima, enclosing our sales proposal. Once the request is signed off on by Kallima, Jorryn will free up funds, which can be paid out according to a PO from our offices.

Once you've created this document, you should share it with your initial contact to confirm that the campaign makes sense.

Note: There is no need to make your sales campaign document a vast tome. In fact, you're better off if it's short, because then it will be easier to edit as you inevitably learn more while moving forward with the opportunity.

Schedule Activities to Match the Decision Process

You now have a model that allows you to tailor your selling activity to the customer's buying process. Go through your list of activities and schedule them based on the prospect's current stage.

Resist the temptation to jump forward in the process. Let the opportunity develop at the customer's speed. If you try to force the issue, you'll only delay the overall process, because you'll end up raising issues that aren't appropriate at that stage.

Getting involved in a complicated discussion of the cost of your software (stage 5) is absurd if you haven't yet built consensus about the financial impact of the problem that it's supposed to solve. For example, an engineering firm using a decade-old CAD system could know that their engineers might be more productive with a modern system, but still not be sure whether an upgrade would save $100 a day or help them earn new business worth $10,000 a day.

It's a mistake to spend too much time defining a solution until the prospect has actually decided to spend some money.

As you move through the opportunity, update the document as you learn more. You'll find that if you keep your sales campaign documents current, you'll be able to juggle more opportunities at one time, and that means more sales and more commissions for you.

Where to Go from Here

When it comes to understanding the buying cycle, I can definitely recommend Mark Sellers. He's a really dynamic guy, with lots of good ideas. He can be reached through www.funnelprinciple.com. His book is *The Funnel Principle: What Every Salesperson Must Know About Selling* (self-published, 2008).

CHAPTER 12

HOW TO BUILD CONSENSUS TO BUY

Throughout the development of the opportunity, you'll be meeting one-on-one (or in very small groups) with various individuals who can help or hinder the purchase of your offering. In most cases, you won't be giving a sales presentation or a sales pitch.

Instead, you'll be having conversations that will clarify your understanding of the company's goals and problems, gathering information to help you better position your offering, and helping to build consensus that purchasing your offering makes sense.

You may also be asked to give presentations to larger groups or to give demonstrations, which are covered in subsequent chapters. For now, let's look at the basic types of decision makers and the roles that they'll likely play as you move forward with the opportunity.

In B2B selling, decision makers tend to fall into one of three categories:

- **Operational managers** run departments and are responsible for making things happen in those departments. Operational managers are typically the "owner" of a problem that your offering will solve, or the "owner" of a goal that your offering will allow the manager's department to achieve.

- **Technical gurus** are highly trusted individuals who (typically) could be in management but prefer to remain inside engineering or manufacturing. Technical gurus are often the operational managers' chief advisers. In some cases, they may actually have more clout than the operational manager both inside or outside the manager's organization.

- **Executives** consist of the corporate officers who run the company. They're usually not very involved in day-to-day operations, but tend to have ownership of broad areas of responsibility. They almost always have both an official agenda and a hidden agenda. The following table shows the most common scenario:

Title	Official Agenda	Hidden Agenda
CEO/President/ Chairman	The stock price or (if privately held) the exit strategy.	How the stock price impacts the exec's compensation mix.
COO	Smooth running of the various parts of the corporation.	Positioning to become the CEO.
CFO	Financial health (profitability) of the company.	Also positioning to become the CEO.
CMO/VP of Manufacturing	Reducing inventory, eliminating waste, decreasing costs.	No hidden agenda, the basic job is already challenging enough.
CSO/VP of Sales	Creating an environment for profitable selling.	Keeping his job when the forecasts are missed.
CTO/VP of Engineering	Generating innovative product ideas.	Keeping the engineers happy and productive.
CIO	Provide data processing services to the company.	Appearing to be as important as the other C-level executives.

That's the basic lay of the land. However, if you're going to move the sale forward, you'll need to be able to communicate with each type of decision maker, in the language that that decision maker understands. Furthermore, you'll need to flesh out the basics given above in order to build a case for purchasing your offering.

Research the Decision Makers

When you meet with decision makers you have two goals, one of which is dependent on the other:

- Goal 1: Have a productive conversation that helps the decision maker see that purchasing your offering aligns with her agenda.

- Goal 2: Get that decision maker to make some kind of public endorsement that the purchase will take place. Such endorsement can be anything from agreeing to a demonstration to writing an email requesting that other decision makers meet with you. Obviously, this is an unlikely outcome if you don't achieve Goal 1.

In order to have a productive conversation, you need to know more about each decision maker than can be encapsulated in your sales campaign document. To thoroughly research a decision maker, you can draw on both public and private sources.

Public sources include a company's financial statements, press releases, conference proceedings, annual reports, published interviews, and so forth. Start your research by gathering enough public information to get an overview of the target firm, as well as its basic strategies and challenges. This gives you context to better understand the specifics of the decision maker's roles and responsibilities.

Private information is what you can glean from conversations with insiders such as your initial contact and anyone else who might know the decision maker (former employees, customers of the decision maker's firm, mutual colleagues, etc.). Your overall goal is to understand as much as is practical to gather (given whatever time constraints you're under) so that you can have a productive conversation with that decision maker.

For example, suppose you're selling gravel crushing equipment to a mining company. Your initial contact is a line engineer who works in the masonry supply group. He explains that:

- Decisions about how to use excess stone would be made by the Director of Auxiliary Products.

- Equipment-purchasing decisions are made by the VP of mining operations.

- The chief mining engineer is consulted on all equipment and manufacturing decisions.

- The CFO has to sign off on all deals involving more than $10,000.

In order to make this sale, you will need to meet with all these people. To prepare, delve into the company's operations and finances so that you can talk intelligently about the benefits of crushing gravel and selling it, rather than disposing of it. The best sources of this information are the company's website and, if publicly held, whatever publicly available documents they file with the government of the country in which they're incorporated. In the United States, this is the Securities and Exchange Commission (www.sec.gov).

As you research each decision maker, determine how they might be approached. Some of this will be obvious; the CFO, for example, will want to know the ROI. However, you are also looking for additional information that might help you better understand how to sell to that individual.

For example, suppose you discover that that VP of mining operations has only come to the United States, from Germany, two years ago. Business is conducted more formally in Germany, so you'll want to be extremely meticulous in your appearance and conduct yourself with more reserve than with the chief mining engineer, who is a Texan who shows up to work wearing a bolo tie.

You're also looking for any perspectives about how each decision maker approaches business decisions. For example, with the CFO, it will be useful to know how she thinks about ROI. If she's shown, in the past, a tendency to make decisions based on short-term opportunities, you will probably want to present an ROI case that shows profitability in one year rather than five years.

Here's a useful technique that shows how to create, within ten minutes, a short document that tells you most of what you need to know about a decision maker in order to have a productive sales meeting:

- **Step 1: Go to Hoovers.com** (a site that compiles information on companies and executives). Do a search on the corporate name. Unless the company is very small or very closely held, you'll likely get a summary of the company and its business model, the basic financials, and the names of a few top executives, even if you don't have a subscription. If there's no listing for the prospect in Hoovers, skip to step 3. If there is a listing, cut and paste the summary and the headquarters address into the top of your profile document. If the company is not publicly held, skip to step 3. If it is publicly held, continue to step 2.

- **Step 2: Go to www.sec.gov.** Click on "Search for Company Filings," then "Companies and Other Filings." Enter the prospect's corporate name. You'll get a list of documents. Click through to read their most recent 10K and 10Q reports. Typically you get a list of .html files. Click on the first one, which will contain the bulk of the company's last detailed financial report. The most important sections are the financial tables, the list of executives, the descriptions of the prospect's business model, and the "issues and uncertainties." This last identifies the prospect's pain points that might provide an opening for a sale. Cut and paste whatever looks interesting into your profile document.

- **Step 3: Go to the company website.** Click on the "About" link and examine everything that the company has to say about itself. Pay particular attention to any management biographies. Cut and paste whatever looks interesting into your document. Look under "News" (or "Media Relations" or similar) for the prospect's recent press releases. Cut and paste any releases that look interesting from the perspective of your firm's offerings. Now look under "Jobs Available" (it might be called something else) to find out who they're hiring; that gives you a good idea of how and where they're planning to expand and where they're short of resources.

- **Step 4: Google the corporate name and the name of the decision maker.** (Hint: Put both in quotes like so: "John Doe" "Acme Corp.") Look over the first two pages of results. (Look at the links and the summary.) If there's a profile on Facebook, LinkedIn, or Plaxo (business social networking sites) examine the contents. If not, look for news articles and other sources. Take special note of anything like references to a personal life or conference speaking engagements. Cut and paste whatever looks interesting into your profile document.

- **Step 5: Save your draft document.** If you need more information, contact people who know that decision maker and will share information about him. Update the document as necessary. Add any personal information that comes up, like birthdays and anniversaries. Review the document every time you meet with that decision maker and use the information to better show how you can help the decision maker achieve his goals.

Meet with the Decision Makers

Now that you know to whom you're selling, set up meetings with the decision makers. During these meetings strive to have a productive conversation that shows you've done your research, and that you've got a solution that addresses their problem.

You will not typically go into a decision maker's office and talk about your offering's features and functions. Instead, build on your basic sales message by relating what you have to offer to the needs and agenda of the individual decision maker. Here's an example of how to approach this conversation using the earlier example of the gravel crusher.

HOW TO SAY IT

Director of Auxiliary Products: Hello, please sit down.

You: I think I may have found a way to increase the revenue of your division by 25 percent.

DAP: How so?

You: Right now you're discarding about 200 tons of stone waste a day. If you added a gravel crusher 100 feet from the mine entrance, you would not only reduce your drayage cost, but you'd have a product that could be sold at $100 a ton.

VP of Mining Operations: Greetings. I have heard good things about you and so have agreed to meet with you.

You: I'm very conscious that you are a busy man and truly appreciate the opportunity to speak with you.

VPMO: Please proceed.

You: I recently had a conversation with your Director of Auxiliary Products. We estimate that your firm could save 2 million a year in drayage costs and make an additional 30 million in revenue, by opening up a line of gravel products. My company makes a gravel crushing machine that can handle that load and we are willing to handle the details of setting up the buyers for your products.

VPMO: This is very interesting. How much does your machine cost?

CFO: I'm very busy. I've heard you want us to buy some equipment?

You: I've been working with your VP of Mining Operations and your Director of Auxiliary Products to define a spin-off business that will achieve an ROI within six months. Here's a spreadsheet showing the initial expense and the expected incremental revenue.

CFO: I'll be happy to look this over, but if what you say is true, it sounds like a no-brainer.

Chief Mining Engineer: What's this I hear that you're planning to put one of them gravel crushers on our line?

You: Actually, I was hoping that you would be able to tell me whether it's possible to introduce a machine like that without disturbing the rest of the operation.

Chief Mining Engineer: Well, it might be tricky. Do you have the specs?

You: Certainly. I also have one of our design engineers on call so he can answer any questions that are too technical for me. Does anything strike you at first glance as a problem?

Your goal in each meeting is to get the decision maker to make a public commitment to approving the purchase. Public commitments can range from an email sent to the entire company to agreeing to attend a meeting where the project will be discussed.

What's important here is to get the decision makers involved in moving the decision forward. You want the decision makers to "own" the decision to buy, so that over time the purchase becomes, literally, a "done deal."

A Word About CEOs

Selling to CEOs is a bit different than selling to other decision makers, especially when the company is very large. Big company CEOs tend to believe:

1. My time is incredibly valuable.

2. I am an important resource.

3. I easily make difficult decisions.

4. I am worth the big money I make.

Some sales professionals wrongly believe that the way to talk to a bigwig CEO is to truckle. Nothing could be further from the truth.

The *only* way to talk to a large company CEO is as an equal. If you're going to be effective selling to a CEO, you've got to believe that your time is valuable and you are an important resource (and so forth). If you don't believe these things about yourself, then don't bother calling on CEOs, because they will sense that you're an underling and treat you accordingly. (As in: "Please don't bother me; talk to some junior manager.")

That being said, it should be noted that big company CEOs (and some small company ones, too) have a tendency to play mind games. For example, a friend of mine once had a meeting with a very famous CEO to discuss a real estate acquisition. The story he told me about the negotiation is a perfect example of how CEOs try to intimidate people.

The meeting was held at the famous Trump Towers in New York City. My friend, though savvy at business, found it impossible not to be awed by the fact that he was riding the elevator featured in the television show *The Apprentice*.

Rather than meeting immediately with the CEO, my friend was taken to a conference room to discuss the final terms with some staffers. A message was then brought to the meeting that the CEO would be arriving in a few minutes. A staffer took my friend aside and said: "You need to understand that the CEO never shakes hands with anybody. So don't be offended if he doesn't offer his hand, and don't offer your hand when he comes in the room."

While my friend digested this tidbit, the staffer continued: "Our CEO is a very busy man and prefers to make decisions quickly. So if the meeting lasts less than five minutes, please don't take it amiss, because that's normal for him."

Finally, the bigwig makes his appearance. He walks right over to my friend and warmly shakes his hand. Then the CEO proceeds to spend forty minutes with my friend, discussing the business and then, at last, ironing out the final terms. And those terms were, as you probably guessed, less advantageous than my friend might have hoped.

When my friend told me this story, he kept talking about how impressed he'd been. "He even shook my hand!" he said, taking that as a sign of special privilege. My friend had absolutely no idea that he had been totally mindgamed. Here are the specific games that Trump played with him:

- **Game 1: The Impressive Office.** CEOs have impressive offices because they want you to be awed. If you are, you're being just as gullible as a teenage girl who's impressed because a guy has a neat car. To his credit, my friend saw through this one.

- **Game 2: The "He's Too Busy" Routine.** CEOs sometimes make you wait to see them, even if you have an appointment, in order to make you feel that the CEO and her desires are more important than your time and your desires.

- **Game 3: The Underling Gauntlet.** CEOs often use underlings to make you feel like an underling. If you're not careful, you end up feeling "socially" bonded to the underlings and thus in a subservient position while meeting the CEO.

- **Game 4: The Unexpected Handshake.** The first three games are pretty common in CEO land. This one is new to me, so I guess it's something that Trump thought up himself. Trump is turning a common business courtesy—the handshake—into a negotiation advantage.

- **Game 5: The Meeting Extension.** CEOs often set low expectations of the amount of time they'll be spending, so that people feel complimented if they spend more than that amount. Trump probably had an hour blocked off anyway, because this was a fairly significant business deal.

The lesson here is that when you're selling to CEOs, don't get caught up in their exalted self-image. Consider: You have something the CEO needs and the CEO has something you want. So the two of you are equally important.

Otherwise, selling to a CEO is just like selling to any other decision maker, with the proviso that you need to address the CEO's agenda, which is typically "big picture" stuff like the stock price, business partnerships, mergers, the investment community, and so forth.

Let's suppose you were asked to meet with the CEO of the mining firm, prior to getting the order. Your conversation might sound something like this:

HOW TO SAY IT

CEO: Remind me why you're here.

You: I've been working with your team to build up the gravel business that will add $20 million in revenue.

CEO: We're a $1 billion a year company. Why should we bother?

You: Actually, there's another aspect of this that might be of interest to you. I understand that there may be additional regulatory pressure put on mining firms?

CEO: Yeah, that's a big headache for us.

You: Launching a gravel business will not just make you money. It will also allow you to brag about being environmentally friendly, since you'd be recycling waste product.

CEO: That might be useful. Have other companies been able to position it that way?

Where to Go from Here

My favorite expert in this area is Keith Eades. His book is *The New Solution Selling* (McGraw-Hill, 2004). Another excellent book is Jeff Thull's *Mastering the Complex Sale* (Wiley, 2010). Both are definitely worth reading. Keith can be reached through www.spisales.com, and Jeff through www.primeresource .com.

CHAPTER 13

HOW TO GIVE A B2B SALES PRESENTATION

When most people start out to create a B2B presentation, they start with the question "What do I want to say to these people?" That's the exact wrong question to ask. The presentation is not about what you're saying but "What decision do these people really need to make?"

In the early stages of a sale, the required decision might be "to form a working group to analyze the problem more fully." By contrast, in the late stages of sales, the required decision is likely to be something more like "Is there sufficient reason to buy this offering?" All of these are variations of the larger decision, which is "Should I buy this offering?"

Buying decisions are always the result of change in the decision maker's emotional state. Prior to making a decision, an audience does not feel that a decision is necessary. Not yet. Then something happens in the audience's emotional state that brings the matter to a head. The audience now feels that a decision MUST be made.

At that point the audience (i.e., the decision makers in the audience) decides. A persuasive presentation is what changes the audience's emotional state to make them feel that a decision must be made—*right now.*

In business there are six emotional keys that unlock that all-important decision-making process. They are:

- **Key 1: Greed.** "If we make a decision now, we'll get a big reward."

- **Key 2: Fear.** "If we don't make a decision now, we're basically toast."

- **Key 3: Altruism.** "If we make a decision now, we're good people."

- **Key 4: Envy.** "If we don't make a decision now, the other guys will win."

- **Key 5: Pride.** "If we make a decision now, they'll know we're smart."

- **Key 6: Shame.** "If we don't make a decision now, they'll know we're dumb."

Truly persuasive presentations contain all six of those emotional keys, because it is only under the pressure of these emotions that any decision will be made. The underlying drivers behind these emotions are, of course, pain and pleasure. Truly persuasive presentations play on the six key emotions to:

- Raise the likelihood of pain and lower the likelihood of pleasure if a decision *is not* made.

- Raise the likelihood of pleasure and lower the likelihood of pain if a decision *is* made.

When these expectations are set, a decision is *inevitable.*

Research Your Audience

While the six emotional keys (and the pain and pleasure behind them) completely drive the decision-making behavior, the actual decision making always takes place within the context of a belief system. For example, if a company sees IBM as their main competition, the "fear" and "envy" segments are best stated in terms of competing with IBM.

If you are going to create the emotions that drive decision making, you need to know not just the audience's current emotional state but also the beliefs that they're using to evaluate the emotional weight of anything that you might present to them. And that means research. The more thoroughly you research your audience, the more likely you'll be to understand their current state and the better you'll marshal emotions to change that state.

It is in this context—finally—that information becomes important. Even though your presentation is intended to change emotions, because this is the business world, that emotional change will result from the expression of new information and the reframing of old information. Remember, however, that it is not the information that is important, but the emotional effect that your use of the information has on the audience. This is an important distinction.

For example, suppose you're trying to sell an inventory control system to a high-tech firm. You learn, as the result of your research, that (1) they've been dinged by investors for having high inventories, and (2) their main competitors have just implemented a "just-in-time" inventory system. That's just information. What's important is the *emotional effect* that those two facts will have when juxtaposed with one another—based on the prospect's belief system.

Let's suppose your research also reveals that your prospect's CIO was just replaced and the new CIO was promoted from the ranks. That's more information, but what's important is that the new CIO may lack confidence and possibly be risk averse. This information also provides clues into how you can base your presentation's emotional content around that new CIO's belief system (i.e., "If I screw up, I'll lose this job").

Craft a Story That Matches the Audience

A story is a sequence of events that has emotional consequences.

The human brain organizes *everything* into stories, because that's how we understand the meaning and context of everything around us. Because of this, a persuasive presentation *always* tells a story.

It is this story that harnesses the power of the six key emotions, thereby changing the emotional state of the audience, so that a decision *must* be made. Here are the rules:

1. *The story starts with a "heart-stopper."* Every movie, TV show, or novel starts with something that captures your attention (i.e., captures your emotions) and holds your interest while you get into the story. Without a heart-stopper, the audience's mind will wander.

2. *The story is about the audience . . . not about you.* The story connects emotions to the audience's current situation so that a decision becomes inevitable. You (or your firm) can play a "best supporting actor" role, but the main role is always the audience and what happens (or might happen) to them.

3. *The story ends with a "risk-remover," then a "close."* The risk-remover eliminates any remaining reluctance to make a decision. The close pushes the audience over the edge and essentially forces them to make the decision, *right now.*

HOW TO SAY IT

Let's suppose you're presenting an inventory control system to a group of decision makers, influencers, and stakeholders. The purpose of the presentation is to help build wider consensus that the budget allocated to the problem your offering solves should be directed to purchase your offering.

You would typically give this type of presentation *after* you've worked with your initial contact and some of the decision makers to flesh out your proposed solution and to confirm that it makes sense. Like ALL effective sales presentations, it is not a sales pitch; it is a means of building wider consensus within a larger group of people.

Please note that the slides should be exactly as shown, with no detail or bullet points. Presentations with bullet points (and where the presenter "reads" them) are generally ineffective. Instead, put the important piece of data—the one that will serve the purpose of the presentation—on a single slide.

Slide	Script
$10 million	(Pause for five seconds.) Yes, $10 million. That's what you lost last year.
Inventory Problems	According to the research that I've conducted with your team, your company's inability to track inventory has resulted in the defection of three large customers and several smaller ones. The total amount of revenue from those accounts was $20 million, but the reputation that you've gotten in the industry has lost you additional sales. In fact, $100 million is probably a conservative estimate.
Lost Market Share	If the current trend continues, there's no doubt that you will be losing marketing share to your competitors. This will allow them to apply economies of scale that your company will eventually be unable to match. Worst case, you could go into a downward spiral where you become successively less competitive.
Controlling Inventory	The challenge with inventory control isn't just getting costs under control; it's turning your inventory into a competitive advantage. Here are some examples of companies that have not just managed to reduce their inventory costs, but used a shortened supply chain and just-in-time inventory to gain new customers . . .
[Simple Table]	Here is the top line of a spreadsheet that I've worked up with the help of Joe in accounting that shows how an inventory control solution can gradually get expenses in line and increase sales revenue. You'll note that the bulk of the cost savings comes within three months of installation, but then there's a follow-on effect of increased revenue.

Slide	Script
Return on Investment (ROI)	The most attractive element of this solution is that it virtually pays for itself within the first three months. Note that this ROI does not include the incremental revenue that you'll be making in years two and three.
Next Steps	As soon as we get the go-ahead, we can have this system installed within three weeks. I've already met with your technical guru to ensure that it's fully compatible with your existing infrastructure and our engineers have prequalified your system for an easy install.
Questions	I'm happy to answer any questions you may have.

Note that this story:

- Opens with a heart-stopper.

- Maximizes the pain of not making a decision.

- Maximizes the pleasure of making a decision.

- Appeals to most of the six key emotions.

- Is mostly about the customer rather than your offering.

- Reduces the risk by focusing on a quick ROI.

Needless to say, you will need to have plenty of real data behind the various points in the story, and you may need some backup slides in case a member of the audience wants to "drill down" into your assumptions. However, the point of the structure is creating emotion and persuading the audience to take the next step—whatever that might be.

Tell the Right Story in the Right Way

Stanford professor Stephen M. Kosslyn (who was formerly chair of the Harvard psychology department) has developed "Cognitive Communication Rules," which in turn lead to specific recommendations. Based on the most important of those recommendations, he provided me with the following guidelines for making sure that your presentations are effective:

- **Prepare anew for each audience.** Human beings share common desires and dreams, but beneath the commonalities are differences specific to individual situations. Every industry has unique needs, and every company in every industry has unique needs, and every group of customers in every company has unique needs. For your presentation to become a relationship-building event and move the sales process forward, it must address what's important to the individual customer and must provide that information at the appropriate level of detail.

- **Use examples relevant to the audience.** Make sure your presentation uses terminology that will be meaningful to that customer. Use proof points and illustrations that resonate with that customer's business experience. If you're presenting to a group with varied levels of expertise, aim for the middle ground when you target the level of detail. Don't aim for the lowest common denominator. There's no presentation blunder bigger than boring the bulk of the audience.

- **Don't just tell . . . show and tell.** If you present information with both words and pictures, you'll have twice the impact, because the information will be stored in twice as many places. Combine both text and graphics in your slides when you want to make an important point. The combination will help your audience remember what you're trying to communicate and help them fit it into the bigger picture of their working environment.

- **Mix it up.** If every slide looks the same, you risk boring the audience. Vary your slides so that some contain just words, some contain just pictures, and save the punchy "words and picture" combo for your most important points. Hint: a video clip in the midst of a presentation creates a sudden burst of movement. This accesses yet another area of the human brain, making your presentation (literally) more memorable.

- **Plan how to direct the audience's attention.** To make sure the audience is following your arguments, make important elements larger and brighter (or louder). Provide an outline structure to help the audience understand where those elements are in the overall message. If you need your customers to understand something complex—like a multi-tier supply chain diagram—build the slide one part at a time, showing only the part that you're discussing at each point in the presentation.

- **Don't overwhelm.** There's a natural tendency, when giving a presentation, to provide so much information that it's abundantly clear that you know everything there is to know about the subject matter. Unfortunately, this kind of "information dump" forces the customer to sort through the data and figure out what's really important—if they don't simply tune you out. Your presentation should provide as much information as is needed to support your story—nothing more.

- **Use a full range of communications options.** Don't let the ease of making bulleted lists in PowerPoint slides lull you into thinking that bullets are always best. A personal anecdote or telling example is often much more effective than anything that you can display on a screen. Think of your PowerPoint slides not as "the presentation" but as a visual aid to "the presentation," which consists of YOU communicating with customers.

- **Build in breaks.** Nobody likes being force-fed. If a presentation is longer than a few minutes, you should build in "breaks" that give the audience time to digest what's already been said. A break might consist of a cartoon or a joke, providing they are relevant to the presentation. A video clip illustrating an important point can also break up the rhythm, and help aid retention.

- **Prepare for questions.** Even though you've told the story, an active and involved Q&A period often leads naturally to next steps in the sales cycle, like additional appointments, additional contacts, and even closing the deal. To make sure that you have a productive Q&A, anticipate questions that might come up—and leave those bits out of your presentation.

Rehearse, Then Go for It

Once you've built your presentation, rehearse it at least three times to make sure you're ready to go in front of a live audience. Then, when you give the presentation, follow these five common-sense rules:

- **Rule 1: Don't hand out copies.** If you distribute a hard copy of your slides before your presentation, the audience will read ahead and try to guess what you're going to say. This will force you to remove any accidental misinterpretations prior to communicating your real message and also weaken the emotional impact of what you're trying to say.

- **Rule 2: Keep your slides in sync.** You don't want your audience reading something on the screen that's different than what your mouth is saying. To prevent drifting, make sure each slide contains only as much as you can read aloud or describe in about one minute. (More than that, and either you'll wander, or the customer's attention will wander.)

- **Rule 3: Talk *to* the audience, not *at* them.** A persuasive presentation should be like a conversation between friends or colleagues, not like a soapbox speech or a sermon. Relax. Breathe. Use the same tone of voice that you'd use in a one-on-one conversation. Let your eyes meet the eyes of the various members of the group. Tell your story the way you'd tell it at a dinner party.

- **Rule 4: Don't focus on your notes.** If you're constantly looking down at your notes, the audience will see your eyes staring downward—a primal image of embarrassment. Worse, the audience will follow your gaze and focus their attention on what you're focusing on. In that case, their most vivid memory of your presentation might be the back of your laptop or the back of the podium.

- **Rule 5: Direct the audience's attention.** At times, your presentation will direct the customers' attention to what's displayed on the screen, like when you're discussing a graph, or following step-by-step through a logical argument. Other times, you'll want to direct their attention to what you're saying and how you're saying it. In this case, the slide might merely introduce an anecdote with a title or an appropriate, reinforcing graphic.

Where to Go from Here

If you're looking to learn more about the psychology of sales presentations and adapt your presentations accordingly, I recommend Stephen M. Kosslyn's excellent books *Clear and to the Point* (Oxford University Press, 2007) and *Better PowerPoint* (Oxford University Press, 2011). He can be reached through Stanford University, where he is the Director of the Center for Advanced Study in the Behavioral Sciences.

CHAPTER 14

HOW TO GIVE A B2B PRODUCT DEMONSTRATION

A product demonstration does more than just prove that the product exists and that it works as advertised. When done correctly, a product demonstration allows the prospect to see and feel, at a gut level, how things will be different after they've bought the product. As such, it can be a powerful sales tool.

A great product demonstration captures the imagination and holds it. Ideally, it turns the *very idea of not buying* into a sad state of affairs. Because of this, the idea of a "one size fits all" demonstration is completely ridiculous. Every prospect is unique, so every demonstration must be uniquely matched to that prospect.

And that means the same kind of internal and external research that you performed when you were looking to cultivate individual decision makers. Use public sources, like the company's SEC filings, press releases, conference proceedings, annual reports, published interviews, and so forth to understand the context of the demonstration, and then gather some specific information about the people or group who will be viewing the demonstration.

This should not be difficult, because you have already done this kind of thing to get to the point where you're being asked to demonstrate. However, it does make some sense to revisit the issues, because you want your demonstration to be in line with how you've presented the product and to tell a similar story—the customer's story, not *your* story.

Tell the Customer's Story

A product demonstration should never be a tour of features and functions. The product demonstration should always tell a story, using the product as the visual hook that makes the story real.

The story you tell is the prospect's story, with the prospect as the hero who must overcome an obstacle in order to achieve a goal. In your demonstration, the product is the "magic sword" that helps the prospect, the key element that makes their success possible.

The demonstration also frames that story in a way that makes sense, not just to the prospect's business, but to the individual goals and desires of the people viewing the demonstration.

HOW <u>NOT</u> TO SAY IT
Suppose you're demonstrating an inventory supply system. The worst thing you can do is give this kind of demonstration:

> **You**: On the top menu, you can open files, save files, set preferences, and convert to other formats. The next menu is the edit menu, where you can copy, cut, paste, and insert. When you copy, you highlight the portion you want to copy and then paste it where you want it. Note that you can do this with any inventory record. On the next menu . . .

HOW TO SAY IT

Instead, tell a story that fits the way the individual viewing the demonstration thinks about their business. For example, if you're demonstrating the inventory control system to a manufacturing director, you know (from your research into his role and his industry) that his concerns include lost inventory, excess inventory, and warehouse space. Here's how to say it:

> **You:** Imagine that a call comes in from your plant that they've almost run out of component parts and will have to shut the line down if they don't get more within two days. All you need to do at this point is query the system (like so . . .), which now locates any excess inventory at your other plants as well as your key suppliers. Voilà! You select a new source with a point and click (like so . . .) and the system is already printing shipping orders and labels so that the needed inventory arrives tomorrow.

Now suppose you're demonstrating that exact same inventory system to a CFO. Her concerns include cost overruns, cost saving, and auditing accountability. Here's how to say it:

> **You:** Imagine that increased cost of component parts is pushing your profit margins down to single digits. You generate a quick report of costs associated with those parts (like so . . .) and discover that your company is paying extra to have some of them warehoused across the country and FedExed as needed to the manufacturing facility. You check available inventory space (like so . . .) and discover that there's floor space available locally. You redirect shipments of the components (like so . . .), thereby eliminating the intermediate warehouse. Voilà! You just saved $1 million a year, and raised the profitability of the final product by three full percentage points.

Rehearse, Rehearse, Rehearse

Giving a sales demonstration is three times harder than giving a sales presentation. Why? Because with a demonstration, you must simultaneously focus on the prospect, the effect the demonstration is having on the prospect, and the mechanics of the demonstration.

That's why it's utter madness to try to give a demonstration without rehearsing it *at least three times.* You'd be amazed how many sales reps think they can wing it when it comes to demonstrations. The result is always a disaster.

Use the rehearsal process to tune up your overall message and make the demonstration more effective. As you rehearse, here are some rules to keep in mind.

- **Rule 1: Never show a meaningless feature.** Every feature you demonstrate must be tied directly to a prospect's problem or opportunity.

- **Rule 2: Pay attention to the plot.** A perfect demonstration tells a story, with a beginning, middle, and end. Remember: The prospect is the hero, not you, and not your firm.

- **Rule 3: Use the demo as a proof point.** Some prospects are disposed to think of reasons not to buy rather than reasons to buy. A good demonstration "proves" that sales claims are true.

- **Rule 4: Keep it simple, stupid.** Find an appropriate goal (like "show the CFO why the ROI claims are true"). Achieve that and forget about the rest of the stuff the product does.

- **Rule 5. Edit your script.** The "talking" part of your demo must accommodate the rhythm of the product. If it takes ten seconds to execute a feature, you must fill that time with appropriate patter.

- **Rule 6: Pace yourself.** A perfect product demonstration should be seamless, without long pauses and dead spots.

- **Rule 7: Avoid techie-talk.** Even if the audience is technically oriented, don't get too deeply into *how* the product works. Focus on what it does for the prospect.

- **Rule 8: Jettison the biz-blab.** Avoid tired and trite phrases like "best in class," "robust," "bleeding edge," etc. Such phraseology only makes you look foolish.

- **Rule 9: Minimize your activity.** This isn't a piano concerto! Too much activity on your part makes the demo look too complex.

Once you've rehearsed at least three times, and know exactly what to say, you're *almost* to the point where you can present the demonstration.

Test Everything Beforehand

One of the most painful sales-oriented scenes from Hollywood in recent years appears in the film *The Pursuit of Happyness*. In that movie, Chris Gardner (played by Will Smith, who received an Oscar nomination for his performance) simply *must* make a sale of some medical equipment in order to keep himself and his son from becoming homeless. The equipment fails during a key demonstration, causing the sale to be delayed indefinitely.

That film was true to life, because *nothing* in a sales cycle (short of accidentally killing the prospect) is going to kill a sale faster than a demonstration that goes sour. Sales pros like to believe that prospects will be forgiving, and treat a demonstration glitch as "one of those things." *Wrong!*

A bungled demonstration tells the prospect, at a visceral level, that either you didn't adequately prepare (in which case buying from you is probably a mistake) or (worse) you *did* prepare adequately and the product is a piece of crap that fails even under the most forgiving of circumstances.

Never, ever, give a demonstration without a dry run, preferably at the very location where you'll be giving the demonstration. Never assume that the equipment available at a customer site or conference facility will work. As far as practical, bring *everything* you need to do your demo. For example, if you're demonstrating software, if possible use your own laptop, your own projector, your own pointing device, etc.

And always have a backup plan. If the demonstration does encounter technical difficulties, have some other sales-oriented activity that can fill the gap while your engineers fix the problem. You did remember to get them involved, I hope?

When You Demo, Let the Prospect Lead

You probably thought you'd be presenting your entire script when you give your demonstration. But that's not the case.

The trick to giving a useful sales demonstration is to draw the prospect in, and let the prospect guide the demonstration. Your goal is to make the prospect know what it will feel like after they've actually bought the product. Writing multiple scripts—and basing them on research—prepares you to articulately address just about everything that the prospect might bring up.

You can start the demonstration with whatever you think would be of interest, but the purpose of drawing the prospect into the demonstration is to let them take control. Some sales pros intuitively understand this, because they're accustomed to adapting to prospects' needs and interests.

However, you'd be amazed at how many people are annoyed when a prospect tries to take control of a demonstration. It's almost as if they're thinking of it as a dramatic performance and the prospect as an audience member who ought to remain silent.

If you've done your research, just about anything the prospect asks will fall naturally into the patterns of the stories you've created. However, now you and the customer are creating the story together. The more active the participation, the more likely the demonstration will close the deal.

As you're demonstrating, frequently test (with neutral questions like "Does this make sense?") to confirm that the demonstration is achieving its goals.

HOW TO SAY IT

Let's suppose you're demonstrating a medical device that provides basic blood tests for emergency room triage. Here's how you might let the prospect lead:

> **You:** Suppose you're working triage in an emergency room and you need to know whether operating on an unconscious patient will create problems. Does that happen a lot?
>
> **Prospect:** Yeah. Mostly we worry about whether they've taken something that will prevent their blood from clotting.
>
> **You:** Good, because this device handles that very well. When the unconscious patient is wheeled in, you insert this special IV line, draw two CCs of blood, and put the result into this portable processing unit. Is there someone in receiving who's trained or could be trained to do this?
>
> **Prospect:** Yes, we usually have a nurse on hand. Is the IV standard or is there some extra training involved?
>
> **You:** It's a little different but easily learned. Here . . . try it on me. [Hold out arm]
>
> **Prospect:** You sure?
>
> **You:** Yeah. I've done this plenty of times before.
>
> **Prospect:** The needle's shorter than usual.
>
> **You:** That's because research shows that it's easier to raise veins on unconscious patients because they don't tense up.
>
> **Prospect:** We could train our staff on this very quickly.

You: Good. Now we put the tube into the centrifuge, and within three minutes you know whether or not the patient has taken an anticoagulant within the past two hours.

Prospect: Where's the display?

You: Here on the back, so that it's visible to the attending as well as the nurse.

If a demonstration has gone smoothly, make a final check that the prospect has seen (and experienced) what it would be like to own the product. If you get anything that looks like a green light, ask for the next step, which might be another meeting, another demonstration for another person, or whatever you need to have happen at that point to move the sale forward.

However, it must be said that there is often no better point in the sales cycle to ask for the business than after you've given a solid demonstration. The prospect has participated in an imaginative exercise of using the product as if it were already purchased. Because of that, the prospect is already halfway (and more) to purchasing the product.

Where to Go from Here

This chapter came right out of my personal experience demonstrating software products, which was a huge part of my job before I became a full-time writer. Please feel free to contact me if you need any further advice. You can reach me at www.geoffreyjames.com.

CHAPTER 15

HOW TO WRITE A SALES PROPOSAL

B2B selling often involves the writing of a sales proposal. There is a great deal of confusion surrounding the role of a sales proposal, because it's one of those odd situations where what's supposed to be happening is different from what's really happening.

According to the "official story," a sales proposal is a formal response to a document called a request for proposal (RFP). What's supposed to happen is that the customer, after sage deliberation, makes a decision to buy a particular product and then writes the RFP to create a basis for evaluating multiple sellers who might provide that product.

Theoretically, the sellers, using the RFP as a guide, explain their products in a sales proposal. A committee inside the buyer's organization evaluates the proposals against criteria that include functionality, timing, and price, and awards the contract accordingly. The process is fair and impartial, and allows the best solution to be selected out of a range of options.

That's how it's supposed to happen. What happens in the real world is usually quite different. Customers almost never write RFPs by themselves. In almost every case, the RFP is a result of some segment of the customer organization working with a sales professional who's already been cultivating decision makers. The RFP, as written, will inevitably be skewed to make certain that the vendor's product wins.

When the RFP is released, the sales professional who wrote the RFP has already written a matching proposal. That proposal will win unless something unexpected happens. The other sales professionals, from other firms, who write proposals based on that RFP fall into two categories:

- **Clueless.** They wrongly believe the official story and think they have a chance at being accepted, if they write a sales proposal that matches the RFP reasonably well. It will not, and they will end up having spent a lot of time and money chasing a rainbow.

- **Savvy.** They know that the "lock" is in, but believe that they can "unlock" the deal by working directly with the customer to change the RFP, either explicitly (by driving a release of an updated version) or implicitly, by surfacing issues that the RFP doesn't address.

Because unlocking such a deal can take a lot of time and effort, savvy sales professionals only go through this process if the opportunity is large enough and their chance of unlocking it is high. Most of the time, if you didn't write the RFP, your wisest move is to forget about the opportunity. You've already lost.

How to Write an RFP with a Customer

For the purposes of this discussion, I'm going to assume that you're on the inside track and are participating, with the prospect, in the writing of the RFP or (worst case) working with the prospect to alter an existing RFP.

In either case, you want the burden of work to fall upon you, rather than the prospect. You are going to write the RFP as a service to the prospect, and allow the prospect to edit as necessary. Doing as much of the work as possible yourself is to your great advantage because you want as much of your thinking as possible to get into the RFP.

The ideal role of the prospect (from your perspective) is to provide you with inside information about the company that will help you add requirements to the RFP that can only be adequately fulfilled by your offering. For example, if you have a software offering that supports 50 different languages, you want to uncover every example in the prospect's globally dispersed firm where the use of a local language is a statutory requirement.

In order to correctly "load up" the RFP, you therefore need to know three key pieces of information:

1. What's unique about your offering

2. Where your offering is strong

3. Where your competitors' offerings are weak

For example, suppose your firm has a facility that's 50 miles away from the customer and your closest competitor's nearest facility is 100 miles away. The proposal in this case should state something like "the vendor must have a truck on site within 1 hour of a service call request."

Any area where your product is strong should be similarly emphasized. If you have a documented support capability that fixes problems twice as fast as the industry average, make certain that "speed of support" is a major element of the proposal.

Similarly, if you know where your competitor's product is weak, you should build those weaknesses into the proposal as well. For example, suppose you're selling software and your competitor's application has lots of features, but runs very slow. You want the proposal to identify speed as more important than specific features that your product might lack.

As you go through this process, you'll want to build in elements that appeal to the different constituencies that are part of the decision-making process. Engineers, for example, are more likely to see specific product features as important, while financial decision makers will be more interested in ROI.

Please note that while you'll be having inputs into the RFP and may even write the bulk of it, in the end it's a customer document that provides the structure of your response, which is your proposal.

Start with the Executive Summary

Once you've created an RFP and gotten the prospect to agree that it encapsulates the problem that their firm needs to solve, it's time to write the actual proposal. To do this, always begin with the executive summary.

Some sales professionals wrongly believe that the executive summary should summarize the contents of the proposal. As a result, they write the executive summary last, after all the information has been gathered into the body of the proposal. In fact, the executive summary does not summarize the proposal; it summarizes the reasons why the customer should buy from you.

Think of it as an executive briefing—focused on basic issues and bottom-line results. It is your key sales tool and should be written first, in order to set the tone and direction of the body of the proposal. As we shall see, the primary function of the body of the proposal is to offer a detailed solution and substantiation of your capabilities to deliver that solution.

I interviewed Tom Sant (arguably the world's top expert on proposal writing) on this topic. He believes that the executive summary should follow what he calls the "persuasive paradigm":

- **Part 1: The problem/need/goal.** Demonstrate your understanding of the customer's business situation. The definition of the problem/need/ goal is more than a paraphrase of the customer's original requirements.

Instead, it should reflect the results of your research into the customer's situation and should show that you understand their business. Examples: "You have identified a $5 million shortfall in revenue due to lost inventory." "You are seeking to grow your consultancy by 50 percent a year for the next three years."

- **Part 2: The expected outcome.** Describe the potential positive impact on the customer's organization if the problem is solved, the need is fulfilled, or the goal is achieved. Note that this is not a discussion of your solution's features and benefits. Rather, the focus is on the organization and the gains it will achieve from implementing your solution. Examples: "When problem A is solved, you will have 50 percent less downtime . . ." "Achieving goal B will allow you to open your products to new markets . . ." The reason the executive summary must address client-desired outcomes is to create a strong desire to move forward on the part of the decision maker. Focusing on the need gets their attention (part 1), but focusing on the gain sets up attaining their commitment.

- **Part 3: Solution overview.** Provide, for the nonspecialist, a brief overview of the solution that's being proposed. Ideally, each element of the solution should tie back to one of the customer's problems or needs and to one of the desired outcomes. Examples: "We are proposing A because it solves the problem of . . ." "We are proposing B because it provides the following value to your firm . . ."

- **Part 4: The evidence.** This is a brief mention of why you are capable of delivering the solution on time and on budget: quotes from clients, accolades, awards, and so forth.

- **Part 5: The call to action.** Ask for the business. This can be something as simple as "We're eager to work with you." In asking for the business, mention one or two key factors that differentiate you as a vendor and that make you the right company for the client to choose.

Notice that the executive summary does not start by giving your company history or an overview of your product line. The initial focus must be on the customer and what they need. In fact, the name of the customer should appear two or three times as frequently as the name of the vendor.

Avoid putting costs in the executive summary unless the customer has specifically requested that the price be mentioned there. Instead, use the executive summary to make your first presentation of a compelling value proposition—increased productivity, reduced operating costs, increased market penetration, lower total cost of ownership, or some other important measure of gain.

Emphasizing what you can do for the customer and what's unique about your solution creates a perception of value that can raise your proposal above the rest, even if other solutions might cost less.

HOW TO SAY IT

EXECUTIVE SUMMARY

ABC Industrial Vehicles manufactures, sells, and globally distributes specialized industrial and construction vehicles, primarily to channel partners, who rent them out to businesses and construction firms. As ABC's market has matured, your company has faced additional competition from a large number of global firms, some of which have manufacturing facilities in areas far from your own manufacturing facilities. Since many of these specialized vehicles cannot be driven on public roadways, your business model has suffered from high shipment costs. This has forced you to charge more for your products than some of your competitors in order to maintain profitability.

Many of your sales professionals are experienced in this specialized industrial equipment industry and have extensive knowledge about ABC's product set and the products of competing firms. However, you have told us that you lack a standardized, repeatable sales process. Each sales professional creates his or her own individual sales process in order to address opportunities. As a result, it has been difficult for management to assess the pipeline, make forecasts, and generally run the business. In addition, your sales reps lacked the formal business training to fully satisfy the needs of their customers. ABC's management saw this as a major liability since helping those customers to grow their businesses would clearly have yielded increased revenues and channel loyalty.

[Note: The paragraphs below define the "problem/need/goal."]

You have determined that the best way to address this problem is to create a repeatable sales process and an ongoing program to build a greater level of business acumen throughout the sales organization. You expect this process and program to increase sales by 20 percent per year over the next three years.

[Note: The paragraph above defines the "expected outcome."]

We intend to do this in three steps:

- **Initial assessment.** We will interview ABC's sales teams in order to determine the current situation and needs.

- **Course design.** We will build a customized set of courses that will create and reinforce a sales process and provide ongoing business training.

- **Evaluation support.** We will create a steering committee and a method of measuring and analyzing the progress of the training.

[Note: The paragraphs above define the "proposed solution."]

We are confident that this program will both increase forecasting accuracy and result in improved average performance of your sales staff. Our prior experience with customer XYZ leads us to believe that the growth goals that you've identified for this project can not just be achieved but exceeded.

[Note: The paragraphs above define the "evidence."]

We are eager to work with you to implement this solution.

[Note: The sentence above is the "call to action."]

Make the Proposal into a Sales Tool

There is no generic structure for a sales proposal. In most cases, the structure will be determined by the RFP, especially if the prospect has provided a skeleton structure of what they'd like to see in the proposal.

If the prospect has not done so, you should structure the proposal into the "persuasive paradigm" that you used in your executive summary, but with far more detail. For example, in the "problem" area of the proposal, you might include some detailed information about inventory shortfalls. Similarly, in the "solution" area of the proposal, you would include detailed information about your proposed implementation such as schedule, component parts, staffing, etc.

What's most important in the proposal is its ability of the proposal to answer the questions that various decision makers might have. The information that you include is therefore very similar to the contents of the discussions that you had with various decision makers in Chapter 12.

Throughout the proposal, you should state your solution in terms that each constituency understands and accepts. The "evaluators" will be looking for details and evidence about your solution, your experience, and your capabilities. They will want to see detailed explanations of how you will do the work, who you will provide, what prior successful experience you have in this area, which other customers you have done this kind of work for, how you will manage the project, and evidence of your core competency and financial stability.

Regardless of the structure, start each section of the proposal body with a summary statement that indicates what the section will cover and reinforces your key value propositions.

Avoid the mistake of providing information that is too technical or that offers an abrupt, nonpersuasive answer. For example, suppose the customer's RFP contains the question "Do you have 24/7 support?" As a proposal writer, you have three possible responses:

1. Answer yes and move on to the next question.

2. Include pages of technical detail about the mechanics of your support infrastructure.

3. Describe specifically what differentiates your 24/7 support from the competition's and how those differences will reduce the customer's overall costs.

Approach 1 has too little information, while approach 2 has too much. By contrast, approach 3 turns answering a simple question into an opportunity to create the perception of value that will lead to a successful sale.

For each set of constituencies, you need to articulate a business proposition that makes sense to them, in language that they understand. Furthermore, it must tie into the overall sales message that you've been promoting throughout the sales process.

HOW TO SAY IT

Suppose you're selling coaching software and your core sales message is as follows:

The quickest way to improve employee morale and performance is to turn managers into better coaches. ACME Coaching Software helps your managers learn better coaching skills, track the effects of their coaching impact, and evaluate their own coaching performance.

Make sure every chapter or heading in the sales proposal relates back to that core message, but in language that each constituency will understand. For example:

- **Problem definition (target: all constituencies):** ABC Industries has identified a need to increase productivity throughout the marketing department by 25 percent. They've determined that the easiest way to accomplish this is to increase employee morale and provide a deeper level of training in key marketing skills. [more details]

- **Solution definition (target: operational manager):** We propose working with the management team to create meaningful performance metrics, and then installing an ACME Coaching Software system customized to the requirements of the marketing group. [More details]

- **Technical characteristics (target: customer IT group):** The ACME coaching system runs as an on-demand application across the Internet, with support and maintenance provided at ACME's server facility. It will require all PCs at ABC to be connected to the Internet, and use the Firefox browser. [More details]

- **Financial impact (target: the CSO):** Because access to the ACME coaching system is provided as a group license, up-front costs are low, and access to the system can be provided gradually as additional groups come on board. Because of this, we expect to achieve an ROI almost immediately. [More details]

Once again, the specific content will vary according to the problem and the solution being proposed. The main point is that the proposal is neither a technical specification nor a statement of work, but instead a sales document that's intended to move the sales process to the next step.

Because the proposal is a "product" of your firm, make certain that it represents the quality that your firm is offering the customer. Make sure there aren't any glaring inconsistencies in the description of the products or services.

There should be no obvious grammatical errors and an absolute minimum of typographical errors. If boilerplate (standardized material from other proposals) is included, it must be carefully customized to match the customer's own situation.

Be extremely careful to edit any passages that might contain the names of other companies for which the boilerplate was used in the past. Many proposals have been thrown out simply because the proposal writer left the name of one of the customer's competitors in a paragraph lifted from an old proposal.

Make sure to edit out all the biz-blab and useless buzzwords, unless those are words that you hear constantly in the prospect's regular business lingo.

Where to Go from Here

The thinking in this chapter stems from the brilliant Tom Sant, arguably the world's foremost expert on writing winning proposals. His classic book is *Persuasive Business Proposals* (3rd edition, AMACOM, 2011). He founded an organization that teaches these skills: Hyde Park Partners. They can be reached at www.hydeparkpartnerscal.com.

PART FOUR

How to Close a B2B Deal

Here, at last, is the moment of truth. In Chapter 16, you'll learn how to close the deal, by making it the end of a long series of smaller closes. In Chapter 17, you'll learn how to negotiate final terms so both your firm and the customer's firm benefit. Chapter 18 explains how to use the book to make steady incremental improvements on key skills that you've learned.

The goal of this part is thus twofold: to give you the skills that you'll need to make the sale and to give you a way to constantly increase your success at B2B selling.

CHAPTER 16

HOW TO CLOSE A B2B SALE

When selling to consumers, the "close" can be something of a heart-stopping moment. The sales professional must typically discover the courage to "ask for the business" and then learn his fate at the moment of truth.

That kind of drama is relatively rare in B2B selling, because the decision-making process tends to be drawn out and complicated. Often there is not a specific point where the deal "closes." Instead, consensus often eventually builds to the point where a purchase is inevitable.

In cases where there's a formal evaluation process and multiple bids from multiple sellers, there's simply some kind of announcement of who "won"—typically the sales professional who developed the opportunity and wrote the RFP. It's usually somewhat anticlimactic rather than a moment of drama.

This is not to say that you don't need to close the deal . . . only that the closing process is gradual and takes place throughout the buying cycle.

Make Each Meeting into a Mini-Close

This chapter on closing is largely based on a wonderful interview I did with Linda Richardson, founder of the huge sales training firm Richardson, and one of the smartest people I know. I've made a few changes based on input from readers of the *Sales Machine* blog, but most of the ideas are based on instruction she provided me.

The old adage "ABC—Always Be Closing" is often used to promote the hard sell, where you constantly push for a buying decision. The real meaning of "ABC" is that every activity that you do with the prospect should move the opportunity forward in some way.

To make sure this happens, whenever you call on a customer, you should have an objective in mind that is specific, measurable, and appropriately aggressive.

Specific objectives aren't feel-good goals like "I will get closer to the customer"; they're goals that can be easily assessed and measured, such as "I will get a list of the key decision makers" or "I will ask for the business."

Objectives should be aggressive, but appropriate to the stage of the sales cycle. For example, on a first sales call for a complex multimillion-dollar deal with multiple decision makers, it would be overly aggressive to set an objective like "I will close the deal today."

Setting objectives doesn't mean you can't be flexible and adjust the goal while you're in the meeting. But a great closer always has a direction and understands where the meeting needs to go in order to maintain momentum and win the deal.

Here's a list of some of the "closes" that make up a closing strategy and are appropriate at each stage of the buying cycle:

CLOSES AT STAGE 1: PROBLEM RECOGNITION.

- The initial contact agrees that there's a problem.

- The initial contact agrees to sponsor you to her manager.

- The initial contact agrees to another meeting to estimate financial impact.

CLOSES AT STAGE 2: DEFINE ECONOMIC CONSEQUENCES.

- The initial contact agrees on an estimated financial impact of the problem.

- The initial contact provides a list of decision makers who would be interested.

- The initial contact agrees to sponsor you to present the problem to a working group.

- The initial contact supports your request to meet with the economic decision maker and other key influencers.

- You seek verification from the economic decision maker, i.e., the executive sponsor.

CLOSES AT STAGE 3: COMMIT FUNDING.

- The decision makers reach consensus that money will be spent on this problem.

CLOSES AT STAGE 4: DEFINE DECISION CRITERIA.

- The decision makers ask you to create or edit an RFP.

- You test your solution for validation and seek comparisons with competitors.

CLOSES AT STAGE 5: EVALUATE ALTERNATIVES.

- A key decision maker allows you to present your solution to a larger group of stakeholders, who must be brought on board in order to move the deal forward.

- You ask for the business at the conclusion of the presentation.

CLOSES AT STAGE 6: SELECT VENDOR SOLUTION.

- The decision makers select your offering (the actual close).

- You continue to close through the negotiation to contract.

- You make a post-final presentation phone call to your contact for feedback.

Frequently Check That You're on Target

Whenever you're meeting with a customer, keep the customer involved. During the meeting you will (of course) identify the customer's objectives, strategy, decision process, time frames, etc., and position your ideas, products, or solutions to satisfy those needs. That's basic selling.

However, you must also ask "checking" questions to get feedback from the client about what you've said. This allows you to gauge how the customer is responding so you can adjust your strategy accordingly. Most importantly, this checking process will give you the information you need to confidently close.

Effective checking does not involve leading questions such as "Does that make sense to you?" or "Do you agree?" With leading questions, customers will often take the easy way out and nod along, without really agreeing. Instead, ask checking questions such as, "How does that sound?" or "What do you think?" Unlike leading questions, checking questions encourage the customer to provide you with frank, vital information.

HOW TO SAY IT

> **You:** We have a first-rate delivery capability in all key markets. How would that work for you?
>
> **Prospect:** I'm concerned you can't meet our global needs.

You: I understand that you have global needs. Why do you feel we may not be able to meet them?

Prospect: We want feet on the street and you don't have international offices.

You: We understand how important that local presence is. For that reason, we have formed strong partnerships with the top companies in other regions, who are a part of the culture and are there to serve our clients' needs. How does that address your concern?

Prospect: It might, providing you can invoice centrally.

Every time you position your products and services, you should check to get feedback. The best part about constantly checking is that, if you do it correctly, the client will often preemptively close the goal for you (or even the entire sale) by saying something like "So, when do we start?"

Make a Final Check, then Close

If the customer does not preemptively close, then you MUST move to close or you will lose ground and possibly the entire deal.

You've positioned your products or services so that the customer understands how they meet his or her needs up to now. You've used checking to get feedback to make sure there is agreement and understanding. Now come the mechanics of the close.

First, give the decision maker a concise, powerful summary that reiterates the conversation that you've just had. This summary may include benefits of your products or services. Once you've done this, make one final check—not for understanding but for agreement.

The purpose of this final check is to seek a green light to go for the close. The final check also gives the customer the opportunity to bring up any final objections that might interfere with your close. If a final objection surfaces, handle it, and then restate the final check.

HOW TO SAY IT

> **You:** Our worldwide service capability will allow your employees access anywhere they travel, at an 11 percent reduction from what you're spending today. How does that meet your objective?
>
> **Decision maker:** It's the savings I'm looking for, based on what I've heard.
>
> **You:** That's great. To help us move this forward, I'd like to suggest that we meet with the steering committee. How does that sound?

If the decision maker declines, acknowledge that fact and then find out why. As appropriate, make a second effort. Regardless of whether you actually closed, end the meeting with confidence, energy, and rapport to make a positive last impression.

Thank the client for the business or reinforce the desire to work with the client and follow up immediately. If you were not able to close on that objective, come up with a plan to revisit that goal or achieve it in a different way. You may also want to record your fallback position in your sales campaign document.

When you win the business, show energy and appreciation. Follow up immediately and send an email or make a call to document the decision.

If you make your selling effort the execution of a closing strategy, you will create the momentum you need to accelerate closing and increase your close ratio. Closing requires the strategy to control the sales process and the skill to control the sales call and build the relationship.

By the way, another huge difference between B2B selling and B2C selling is that, with B2B, even after you've got the go-ahead, there's often yet another step—the negotiation on final terms. In some cases, this negotiation can actually take longer (and be more taxing) than the sale itself. That's the subject of the next chapter.

Where to Go from Here

As I mentioned earlier, my philosophy on closing comes primarily from Linda Richardson. Her best book, in my opinion, is the huge bestseller *Perfect Selling: Open the Door, Close the Deal* (McGraw-Hill, 2008). That book is a must-read for anybody who wants to make a lot of money selling B2B. She can also be reached through her company's website, www.richardson.com.

CHAPTER 17

HOW TO NEGOTIATE FINAL TERMS

Even after a company has decided to buy something, it's not unusual for there to be a negotiation about final terms. This typically happens when the offering is complex or entails significant levels of risk (and therefore some kind of risk mitigation). Similarly, if there are legal aspects to the deal (as when a B2B sales forges a partnership of some kind), there are likely to be legal points that need to be negotiated.

Negotiations can be frustrating, especially if you already feel as if you've "closed the deal." However, it's a truism that the deal isn't really closed until the final contract is signed, and it's that final contract that will come out of the negotiation process. However, if you've been following the advice in the previous chapters, you'll discover that negotiating final terms is almost a formality.

Previous chapters, in fact, have been laying the groundwork by encouraging you to constantly strengthen your negotiating position—before you ever get to the negotiation table. Specifically:

- You have eliminated or thwarted competitive threats by getting involved in the sale process early and by positioning yourself as the driver of the RFP process. Similarly, you've avoided getting involved in situations where a competitor already has a "lock" on the deal. This puts you in a stronger negotiating position because, if you do this well, the customer will lack a viable alternative to hold over your head.

- You have developed multiple contacts inside the customer firm, and used those contacts to gather and provide a deeper perspective. By now, you probably understand quite clearly the motivations and politics inside the customer's firm, which will make it easier for you to understand why somebody may take a particular position during the negotiation. Example: The CFO wants a major discount, but the amount of money is irrelevant to the operational manager, who just wants your offering right now.

- You have created legitimacy through the consistency of your approach. Having a solid sales message, taking a gradual approach to getting everyone on board, and working through the issues logically as a series of closes creates the impression that you're a thorough businessperson who can be trusted. Because of that, you'll be believed when, during the negotiation, you promise to adhere to your firm's policies (even if they're not to the customer's liking). When you explain why those policies make sense, the customer will be likely to listen and try to understand the logic behind your position.

- You have developed a theme of mutual success by generating a solution that matches the needs of the various decision makers and stakeholders inside the customer firm. To do this, you helped the customer to crystallize needs and visualize the right solution. As such, the customer sees you as a valuable resource and thus more likely to defer on negotiating points that you see as being important.

In short, you've been "negotiating" all along, simply by behaving like a professional B2B salesperson. So you're already well on your way to getting a win-win agreement.

Prepare Before You Negotiate

Before actually sitting down to negotiate final terms, ask yourself four questions (in your own mind if not on paper) that will help you understand where you are now, and where you'll need to get, in order for the negotiation to be successful:

- **Question 1: What are the parameters that need to be negotiated?** Collect and evaluate information on leverage, values, sale prices, competition, and other factors that will affect the negotiation. Example: You know that the CFO greatly desires a three-month ROI, rather than the six-month ROI you've proposed. You are therefore aware that you may either need to adjust the price in order to produce that ROI, or come up with some form of alternative financing, like rent to own.

- **Question 2: What are my realistic expectations for the results?** Temper your aspirations with feasibility based on what your counterpart has in mind, and reassess your expectations as the negotiating progresses. Example: You know that your counterpart expects to pay only marginally more than they paid ten years ago for the same service. You're not going to get double the old price, no matter what. But you might get a 33 percent increase.

- **Question 3: What are my all-important pricing parameters?** When it comes to price, know the deal you want to forge, and be able to justify it as being realistic. Example: You know that the largest discount you can possibly offer to still remain profitable is 15 percent. Because of that, a discount larger than 15 percent is not acceptable under any circumstances.

- **Question 4: Where do I have room to maneuver?** Leave yourself some bargaining room, but make sure you have a plausible rationale for the positions that you take. Example: You know that your installation team is idle right now, so you can realistically offer the customer an immediate installation, if they're willing to pay full price.

Remain Calm as You Negotiate

Once you're clear on the deal you'd like to forge, and know where you've got wiggle room, sit down with the customer and talk about the issues.

As you negotiate, do not allow the prospect to feel as if he can simply dictate terms. That's a recipe for a win-lose outcome, with *you* on the losing end of the deal. Whenever you take a position, be sure you can buttress it with appropriate rationales. Be specific about your facts and don't let the negotiation process become emotional. Remain detached and objective.

HOW TO SAY IT

CFO: We'll need you to offer this at 35 percent below your asking price in order for this deal to go through.

You: I'm sorry, but if we sold it to you at that rate, we'd be losing money on the deal.

CFO: What kind of idiot do you take me for? I know for a fact that you gave Acme a 35 percent discount.

You: That was a one-time situation because we needed a reference account in that industry.

CFO: Why can't we be a reference account?

You: You can; in fact, we'd love it, but you'd be a lousy reference account if we gave you a 35 percent discount, because then we'd have to give everyone else the same discount, which would put us out of business.

CFO: Why should I care?

You: Let's just be practical here. I've already offered the largest discount that's possible. If you're short on money, maybe there's a way we can scale down the deal, or come up with long-term financing, so that it becomes more affordable.

In the above conversation, the CFO's attempts to make the situation personal fail because the sales professional sticks to the facts and explains the reasoning behind the position.

Remember that the purpose of the negotiating process is to reach a contract, and the negotiation isn't over until the contract is signed. Even so, there's a point in every negotiation where the deal is pretty much what it's going to be. If you've found that you've gotten pretty much what you wanted, don't sweat the stuff that you didn't get. When you've reached that point, it's time to stop.

Sometimes last-minute demands magically appear after a negotiation has been completed. They're usually positioned as "deal breakers" but most of the time they're something else altogether—a simple test to ensure that the negotiated deal is the best possible agreement.

Unfortunately, many sales pros simply give in to such demands, because it seems as if the prospect—the person with the money—holds all the power. However, if you followed the steps in this chapter, you've got some counterbalancing power, remember?

Giving in to any last-minute demand is a huge mistake, because this is what's going to happen:

1. Your prospect makes a last-minute demand.

2. You don't want to lose the sale, so you run back to your management to see whether you can get that demand met.

3. After a lot of extra work, you get internal agreement, and then you run back to the prospect with the good news, expecting to close the deal.

4. Surprise! Your prospect now has another, even bigger demand.

5. You run back, and after even more hard work, get agreement.

6. You go back to the prospect, hoping to close the deal.

7. Surprise! Another demand!

8. Etc.

This process continues until your prospect makes a demand that your management can't stomach, in which case one of two things happens. Either the deal falls through, turning your hard work into a complete waste of time and money, or the deal gets signed but is a headache for your firm, usually because it's unprofitable.

What's worse, "special agreements" and "relationship saving" discounts have an annoying habit of becoming public knowledge, spawning demands for similar deals. Over time, that can damage the profitability, and even the viability, of an entire company.

So if last-minute demands crop up, hold firm to your position. In most cases, the customer will be relieved at this confirmation of your legitimacy and will take the demands off the table.

HOW TO SAY IT

You: Well, I think we're done here. We've got the basic terms in place and we have a start date.

CFO: I'll need to check with the CEO to make sure we can go forward. I'll give him a call. [Leaves the room]

CFO: [Returns] He says we'll need you to go 20 percent lower or the deal is off.

You: Gosh, that's too bad, because I've already given you the best price that I can. I'm really sorry that we can't make this happen. [Get up to leave]

CFO: Just a second. [Leaves to make another call]

CFO: [Returns] Let's go forward. The CEO says he just wanted to make sure he was getting the best deal.

Where to Go from Here

I learned the basics of negotiating during an interview with Randall Murphy, CEO of Acclivus R3. He's a great mentor in this area and can be reached through www.acclivus.com. If your offering frequently gets you involved in complex negotiations, you should consider taking a seminar or two that focuses specifically on this issue.

CHAPTER 18

HOW TO MEASURE, MONITOR, AND IMPROVE

If you've worked through this entire book, you now have two things: the basic skill set you need to sell B2B, and a road map of where to go and who to see in order to hone those skills. As you go forward in your B2B sales career, you'll naturally want to get the most out of your workday and the opportunities that you develop. Here are five basic strategies that can help with this process.

Strategy 1: Find Better Leads

If you're calling on the wrong people, you're spending time on "opportunities" that never had a chance. If your leads are higher quality, you're less likely to be calling on the wrong people. A high-quality lead is one that's highly likely to become a customer. Your challenge is therefore to figure out what constitutes a high-quality lead for your offering, and focus on finding more of them.

- **Tactic 1: Hone your criteria.** Go back to Chapter 5 every calendar quarter and review the process of finding qualified leads. Confirm that you're going after the right leads. Revisit your lead scoring mechanism and observe—based on your current experience—whether it's working for you. Make changes as necessary, based on what you've learned.

- **Tactic 2: Enhance your tools.** Periodically revisit the online tools that you're using to find leads, and research companies and individuals. Check sources like *Selling Power* magazine to find out what other firms are using in their sales environments. If your firm has an Information Technology group, make sure they know about tools that you think would be useful.

- **Tactic 3: Revisit your network.** Everything changes, especially in the business world. Friends and colleagues who previously didn't know of any prospects may know of some now. You've also built up a customer base; enlist their aid in expanding your network and finding new customers. To do this, just follow the instructions in Chapter 2.

- **Tactic 4: Help your marketers.** If you're fortunate enough to have a marketing group that's tasked with generating sales leads, be certain to share with them what you've learned. Provide them with regular, direct information on who's interested and who's buying, along with all the specific details (like job title, industry, typical organizational structure, etc.), so they can get you better leads.

- **Tactic 5: Improve your database.** If you're using a CRM system, it's in your interest to have it current and accurate. Because the CRM system tracks sales efforts, it can provide a treasure trove of statistical data defining the current customer base and how effective you've been. This is one case where doing the (online) paperwork isn't a waste of time.

Strategy 2: Improve Your Prospecting Skills

Even if you're calling on high-quality leads, a certain percentage of them won't be potential prospects, usually because they don't really have a need for your offering, or they do have a need, but no money to buy. As you know, eliminating these "opportunities" from your sales cycle means you'll spend more time with real ones.

- **Tactic 6: Hone your sales messages.** There's no sales message so perfect that it can't be improved. Every few months, try revisiting your core sales message, your elevator pitch, your qualifying questions, and so forth. Based on your current experience, try to make them better, shorter, and more effective. Then test them and see how well they work!

- **Tactic 7: Focus on eliminating more bad leads.** Make certain that you're not falling into the trap of thinking about prospecting as "getting as many as possible into the pipeline." Instead, align your thinking so your initial conversations with a sales lead are not for the purpose of selling, but rather to identify which leads are most likely to become customers—and which are least likely. If you need help, revisit Chapter 10.

- **Tactic 8: Improve your listening skills.** When a potential customer is speaking, listen carefully to what's actually being said, rather than waiting for something that will give you hope of making a sale. For example, if you ask "How would you handle this problem if you didn't have a solution like ours?" and get a response like "We'd probably struggle along for a few more years," the prospect may not be serious about buying.

- **Tactic 9: Remember what's important.** The key issue when developing an opportunity and making a sale is always value. First, the "prospect" must have the budget to buy, or at least some budget dollars that could be spent, if the need is great enough. Second, the prospect must have that need, and the need must have a financial impact that's overwhelmingly larger than the cost of your offering. Anything less, and you'll never be a priority, so you ought to move on.

- **Tactic 10: Reward yourself for disqualifying a lead.** Remember, every lead you *eliminate* from your list is a victory, because it means you won't be wasting your time. Treat the elimination of a lead from your list as much a victory as the conversion of the lead into a real prospect. Celebrate the winnowing process! If you don't, you may find yourself sneaking questionable prospects into the pipeline.

Strategy 3: Increase Your Conversion Rate

Even if you're calling on the right people, if you do or say the wrong things, you'll spend time and money on opportunities that don't pay off. Here's how to help ensure that you don't accidentally lose the deal:

- **Tactic 11: Research the competition.** Once a lead is completely qualified as a prospect, then the prospect is going to buy, either from you or your competitor. Therefore, increasing your "conversion rate" for a fully qualified lead is always a matter of outselling the competition. Ask the prospect who else is calling on them and if there's a threat, accelerate your sales activities to compensate.

- **Tactic 12: Hone your sales campaign document.** The most frequent reason sales reps are outsold is that they didn't talk to the right people— and the competitor did. In many cases, the losing sales rep failed to research and therefore understand the prospect's actual decision-making process, and who would play what role in that process. So don't assume you've got it right from the start. Make changes as you learn more.

- **Tactic 13: Increase the number of meetings.** It's common practice for sales reps to communicate with a senior decision maker at the beginning of the sales cycle, and then revisit that connection at the end of the sales cycle, in order get final approval. However, if your contacts are limited during the middle of the sales cycle, you may lose track of what's going on. Be in regular communication with decision makers so you always know what's changing inside the customer account.

- **Tactic 14: Improve your follow-through.** Many deals have been lost simply because the sales professional forgets to follow up on a commitment. If you make a commitment, log it in your schedule, and make sure that you do it, no matter what. Follow-through is the only way that a potential customer can learn to trust you, and once you've proven you can't be trusted, the likelihood you'll make the sale is effectively zilch.

Strategy 4: Increase the Dollar Value of Each Sale

There is a fixed amount of time and resources connected to every sales effort. While it may take more effort to cut a $1 million deal, it's usually not nearly ten times as much effort as cutting a $100,000 deal. Therefore, the more money you can make on each sales opportunity, the more you'll make overall.

- **Tactic 15: Uncover the entire opportunity.** You must fully develop the customer account during the sales process. This means giving each account your full attention, and spending enough time on it to be able to uncover the full opportunity. By the way, the key to doing this is only focusing on fully qualified prospects, because if you're selling to fewer prospects, you've got more time to dig deep.

- **Tactic 16: Keep doing your research.** In Chapter 11, I explained how to research a decision maker. Continue this research process as you continue to develop the account. That way, you'll be constantly looking for (and finding) additional ways your firm can help that prospect. As you find these, either work to have them added to the current deal, or position them as the next element in your sales campaign after the initial sale has been made.

- **Tactic 17: Use discounts sparingly.** In the case of standard discounts, that drop in margin is already reflected in the business model. However, extraordinary discounts offered merely to secure the sale may not only make the current deal smaller, but (if publicized) can result in discounts (and smaller deals) from future customers.

Strategy 5: Decrease Your Average Sales Cycle Time

The more time that you spend on an opportunity, the less time you have to spend on other opportunities. Here are some tactics for making certain that you're using your time wisely.

There are two types of "time" that are at issue. The first is the *elapsed time* that it takes to move a prospect from initial contact to closing the deal. The second is the *work hours* that you actually spend on that opportunity. Most sales reps focus on the elapsed time, believing that they can influence the customer to buy more quickly.

However, in most cases, the customer already has a time frame in which they intend to buy. Because of this, efforts to "speed the process along" are usually a waste of time. As such, they add to the number of work hours that the rep spends on the account, with no particular payback.

- **Tactic 18: Focus on work hours, not elapsed time.** Focus instead on the work hours that you spend on each account. Find ways to make your interactions with each customer more intense and more productive. Schedule multiple meetings on a single visit. Use web-conferencing to reach remote individuals. Don't reduce the amount of service you're providing; just find a way to spend fewer work hours doing it.

- **Tactic 19: Find the trigger events.** While you're interviewing and meeting with decision makers, try to find out if there is a "compelling event" that will actually trigger the buying process. For example, a prospect might have a certain amount of budget to spend in the current quarter, in which case the compelling event would be the end of the quarter—after which the money will disappear. Similarly, a prospect might be waiting for an order from a large customer before making a purchase of additional components.

- **Tactic 20: Arrange your schedule to match.** As you learn more about your customer's buying process, and the compelling events that will cause them to buy, schedule your activities backward from that event, so you spend the right amount of time (neither more nor less) developing the opportunity. That helps ensure that every moment you spend with the prospect (soon to be customer) is productive.

Any one of the strategies and tactics above will make you a more effective B2B sales professional. However, if you're smart, you'll work on *all five* strategies, because the improvements that they create are like compound interest. (I got this perspective from Donal Daly, CEO of the TAS Group, which has a more formal way of calculating the impact of these incremental changes.) Here's my quick version:

Suppose you spend one day a week prospecting and four days a week selling. Your prospecting results in ten prospects, of which two turn into customers by the end of the week. You spent one day to secure each customer, and two days on the other eight customers who didn't buy. Each of those two customers spends $10,000. Your commission is 10 percent, so you just made $2,000 in that week.

Now suppose you implement the changes above, and still keep to the same basic schedule. Your one day a week of prospecting still results in ten prospects, but they're all highly qualified.

Because you're spending less time on each customer, you manage to close six customers, while four fall by the wayside. Each of those six customers spends an average of $15,000. Your commission is still 10 percent, so you just made $9,000, which is geometrically more than what you made before—for the exact same amount of time and effort!

Where to Go from Here

The guy who had the most influence on my thinking, when it comes to exponential improvement, is Donal Daly, CEO of the TAS Group. He's a big-picture guy who understands how to change sales organizations to make them more productive. He can be reached through www.thetasgroup.com.

ABOUT THE AUTHOR

© 2011 Cathy Colbert

Geoffrey James is best known as the writer of the award-winning *Sales Machine* blog on CBS Interactive's BNET.com. A freelance journalist since 1994, Geoffrey has written hundreds of feature stories for national publications including *Wired, Men's Health, Business 2.0, Selling Power, Electronic Business, Computer Gaming World, CIO, Computerworld, Network World*, and the *New York Times*. He is also the author of several books on business and high-tech culture, including *The Tao of Programming* and *Giant Killers*.

T17.0911